The History of Ivory Coast

From Empires to Independence

Copyright © 2023 by Adeoye Adekunle and Einar Felix Hansen. All rights reserved.

This book was created with the help of Artificial Intelligence and is protected by copyright law. No part of this book may be reproduced or transmitted in any form or by any means, electronic or mechanical, including photocopying, recording, or by any information storage and retrieval system without the written permission of the author, except for brief quotations in a review.

The information and opinions expressed in this book are for entertainment purposes only and are not intended to provide any form of professional or expert advice. The author and publisher of this book shall not be liable for any direct, indirect, consequential, or incidental damages arising out of the use of, or inability to use, the information and opinions contained in this book.

While every effort has been made to ensure the accuracy and completeness of the information presented in this book, the author and publisher assume no responsibility for errors or omissions, or for damages resulting from the use of the information contained herein.

The Land of Abundant Ivory: Ancient Origins 6

The Kingdom of Kong: Early Civilizations 8

Trading with the World: Ivory Coast in Antiquity 11

Gold and Ivory: The Ghana Empire 14

Songhai Influence: The Rise of Ivory Coast 16

Trans-Saharan Trade Routes: Ivory Coast's Role 19

The Arrival of Islam: Faith and Culture 22

Kingdoms Along the Coast: The Akan and Baulé 25

The Portuguese Connection: European Exploration 28

The Era of Slavery: Impact on Ivory Coast 31

Colonial Ambitions: France's Arrival 34

Scramble for Africa: Ivory Coast under French Rule 37

Plantations and Labor: The Colonial Economy 40

From Ivory Coast to Côte d'Ivoire: A Nation Emerges 43

Nationalism and Independence: The Mid-20th Century 47

Félix Houphouët-Boigny: Founding Father and Leader 51

The Politics of Stability: One-Party Rule 55

Cocoa and Coffee: Economic Pillars 58

Challenges of Ethnic Diversity: National Unity 61

The Ivorian Miracle: Economic Growth 64

The Ivorian Civil War: A Nation Divided 67

Post-Conflict Recovery: Reconciliation Efforts 70

Laurent Gbagbo and the Ivorian Crisis 73

Ivory Coast in the 21st Century: A New Dawn 76

Wildlife Wonders: Biodiversity in Ivory Coast 79

Savory Delights: Ivorian Cuisine 82

Grand-Bassam: Colonial Gem by the Sea 85

Abidjan: The Economic Capital 88

Yamoussoukro: City of the Basilica 91

Gagnoa: The Birthplace of Houphouët-Boigny 93

Man and the Dan Culture: A Window to the Past 96

Sassandra: Fishing and Beach Paradise 99

Comoe National Park: A Natural Treasure 102

Conclusion 105

The Land of Abundant Ivory: Ancient Origins

The history of Ivory Coast, also known as Côte d'Ivoire, stretches back to antiquity, when the region was home to diverse civilizations and cultures. It was a land of abundant resources and a pivotal hub for trade, particularly the trade of ivory, which would go on to shape its identity.

The story of Ivory Coast's ancient origins begins with evidence of human habitation dating back thousands of years. Archaeological findings suggest that the region was inhabited as far back as the Paleolithic era, with early inhabitants relying on hunting and gathering for sustenance. These early human communities left behind artifacts, such as stone tools and pottery, providing glimpses into their daily lives.

As time progressed, the fertile lands of Ivory Coast attracted various ethnic groups and cultures. One of the earliest known civilizations in the region was the Kong Empire, which thrived around the 8th century AD. Situated in the northeastern part of present-day Ivory Coast, the Kong Empire was known for its advanced agricultural practices and intricate trade networks. It played a crucial role in the early history of the region. Ivory Coast's name itself alludes to its historical significance as a major center for the trade of ivory. The coast was frequented by Arab traders as early as the 8th century, who sought the valuable tusks of elephants that roamed the lush forests and savannas of the region. Ivory, along with other precious commodities like gold, was in high demand, making the

Ivory Coast a coveted destination for traders. In the centuries that followed, various empires and kingdoms rose and fell in Ivory Coast. One of the most influential was the Ghana Empire, which extended its influence over parts of the region during the medieval period. The Ghana Empire played a pivotal role in trans-Saharan trade, facilitating the exchange of goods, including ivory and gold, with North African and European markets.

Islam arrived in Ivory Coast through trade routes, and it gradually became integrated into the social fabric of the region. Islamic influence left its mark on the culture, art, and architecture of Ivory Coast, as mosques and Islamic traditions became an integral part of the society.

The Akan and Baulé peoples, who inhabited the southern coastal regions, developed advanced societies with rich cultural traditions. These societies were organized around chiefdoms and were known for their craftsmanship in areas such as pottery and textiles.

European explorers, such as Portuguese navigators, began to visit the Ivory Coast in the late 15th century, seeking to establish trade routes to the East and access the region's valuable resources. Their presence marked the beginning of European involvement in the region, which would later lead to colonization.

The history of Ivory Coast's ancient origins is a tapestry woven with the threads of diverse cultures, trade, and the quest for valuable resources like ivory. It sets the stage for the complex and multifaceted history that would unfold in the centuries to come, as European powers vied for control of this rich and promising land.

The Kingdom of Kong: Early Civilizations

In the annals of Ivory Coast's history, the Kingdom of Kong stands as a testament to the thriving civilizations that flourished in the region during ancient times. Nestled in the northeastern part of present-day Ivory Coast, the Kingdom of Kong was a dynamic and influential state that left an indelible mark on the course of West African history.

The roots of the Kingdom of Kong can be traced back to the 11th century, although some historical accounts suggest its emergence as early as the 8th century. It was founded by the Senufo people, an ethnic group known for their agricultural prowess, intricate artistry, and spiritual beliefs. The Senufo established a network of small chiefdoms, which eventually coalesced into the powerful Kingdom of Kong.

The Kingdom of Kong was strategically situated at the crossroads of several trade routes, including those that connected the Sahel region to the coast and others leading to the northern savannas. This favorable geographical position made it a hub for trade and commerce, facilitating the exchange of goods, culture, and ideas with neighboring societies and even distant lands.

Kong's governance was structured around a centralized monarchy, with a powerful king known as the Tiéba reigning over the kingdom. The Tiéba was both a political and spiritual leader, responsible for maintaining order, overseeing justice, and ensuring the well-being of his subjects. The king's authority was bolstered by a council of elders who provided counsel and support in governing the kingdom.

The Kingdom of Kong was renowned for its agricultural productivity. The fertile lands along the Niger River and its tributaries allowed for the cultivation of a variety of crops, including millet, sorghum, yams, and cotton. Agriculture formed the backbone of Kong's economy, providing sustenance for the population and surplus goods for trade.

Trade was a vital component of Kong's prosperity. The kingdom's ivory, gold, and kola nuts were in high demand in the broader trans-Saharan trade network. Caravans traveled from the Sahara and beyond to exchange salt, textiles, and other goods for Kong's valuable commodities.

Religion played a significant role in the lives of Kong's inhabitants. Traditional Senufo religious beliefs, centered around ancestor worship and nature spirits, were deeply ingrained in the culture. The king, as both a political and spiritual leader, had a sacred role in mediating between the earthly and spiritual realms.

Kong's rich cultural heritage extended beyond its religious practices. The Senufo people were known for their exquisite craftsmanship, producing intricate wooden masks, sculptures, and textiles that were both utilitarian and symbolic. These artifacts played a crucial role in ceremonies, rituals, and social gatherings.

The Kingdom of Kong endured for centuries, maintaining its autonomy and influence in the face of external pressures. However, like many African states during the colonial era, Kong eventually fell under French control in the late 19th century. This marked the end of the kingdom's sovereignty and the beginning of a new chapter in Ivory Coast's history.

The legacy of the Kingdom of Kong lives on in Ivory Coast's cultural tapestry, as its traditions, artistry, and history continue to be celebrated and preserved. It serves as a testament to the resilience and vibrancy of ancient civilizations in the heart of West Africa.

Trading with the World: Ivory Coast in Antiquity

In antiquity, the Ivory Coast, also known as Côte d'Ivoire, occupied a prominent place in the intricate web of global trade networks. This land of abundant resources and strategic location along the Gulf of Guinea made it a crucial player in the exchange of goods, ideas, and cultures between Africa and the rest of the world.

The story of Ivory Coast's engagement in trade during antiquity begins with its positioning along the West African coast. Its geographical proximity to the Atlantic Ocean made it an ideal destination for seafaring traders from Europe, Arabia, and beyond. These traders sought the riches that the land had to offer, with ivory being one of the most coveted commodities.

The trade in ivory was the driving force behind Ivory Coast's interactions with the wider world. Elephants, native to the lush forests and savannas of the region, were hunted for their valuable tusks. Ivory, prized for its durability and decorative qualities, held a special allure for traders and craftsmen alike.

Arab traders were among the first to establish links with the Ivory Coast, arriving along the coast as early as the 8th century. Their voyages were driven by a quest for ivory, gold, and other precious resources. These traders facilitated not only the export of Ivory Coast's ivory but also the importation of exotic goods, including textiles, spices, and ceramics, which found their way into local markets.

The trade in ivory was not limited to the coast. Inland, thriving kingdoms and empires like the Kingdom of Kong acted as intermediaries, facilitating the flow of ivory and other goods between the interior and the coast. The Kingdom of Kong, with its centralized authority and control over trade routes, played a pivotal role in connecting the Sahel region with the Atlantic coast.

European explorers, beginning with Portuguese navigators in the late 15th century, were drawn to Ivory Coast in search of new trade routes. They were particularly interested in securing access to the region's ivory, gold, and spices. This marked the beginning of European involvement in the region and the eventual colonization that would follow.

While ivory was a major driver of trade, it was not the sole commodity exchanged. The Ivory Coast was also known for its production of kola nuts, a valued item with cultural significance that was traded throughout West Africa. Additionally, gold, a symbol of wealth and power, was another prized resource that attracted traders to the region.

The trade connections that Ivory Coast established during antiquity had a profound impact on its culture and society. Foreign influences, whether from Arab traders or European colonizers, left indelible marks on the region's traditions, religions, and languages. The exchange of goods and ideas enriched the cultural mosaic of Ivory Coast, shaping its identity as a diverse and dynamic land.

The ancient trade networks that once crisscrossed Ivory Coast's terrain are a testament to the region's historical significance in the global marketplace. Ivory, as both a symbol of wealth and a commodity of desire, played a central role in forging these connections. This chapter illuminates the pivotal role that Ivory Coast played in the tapestry of ancient world trade, a legacy that endures in the nation's cultural fabric.

Gold and Ivory: The Ghana Empire

The history of Ivory Coast is intricately woven with the rise and fall of ancient African empires, and among the most influential of these was the Ghana Empire. While the heart of this empire lay to the north of modern Ivory Coast, its influence extended southward, shaping the region's destiny and laying the foundation for its historical wealth and prominence.

The Ghana Empire, which existed from around the 8th to the 11th century AD, was a West African powerhouse. Situated primarily in what is now southeastern Mauritania and western Mali, it held sway over vast territories and controlled crucial trade routes that connected the Mediterranean world to the rich resources of sub-Saharan Africa, including the Ivory Coast.

One of the empire's key strengths lay in its control of the trans-Saharan trade routes. The Ghana Empire stood at the crossroads of these routes, making it a pivotal trading hub. The most sought-after commodities were gold, ivory, and salt, and Ghana had an abundance of the first two.

Gold, in particular, was a source of immense wealth for the Ghana Empire. The region's gold mines, often hidden in the savannas and riverbanks, were meticulously worked by skilled miners. This precious metal, coveted worldwide for its beauty and rarity, flowed through the trade networks that extended into Ivory Coast and beyond.

Ivory, too, was a prized commodity that contributed to the wealth of the Ghana Empire. Elephants roamed the forests and savannas of the region, providing a steady supply of ivory tusks. This ivory was carved into intricate art and artifacts, some of which were destined for export through the trade routes that passed through Ivory Coast.

Trade was the lifeblood of the Ghana Empire, and its economy was fueled by the exchange of goods with North African traders, primarily Berber merchants who traversed the Sahara Desert. These traders brought with them not only goods like textiles, metals, and ceramics but also the Islamic faith, which gradually spread throughout the region, influencing the culture and religion of the empire.

The Ghana Empire's political structure was characterized by a centralized monarchy, with a powerful king, often referred to as the Ghana, at its helm. The Ghana exercised authority over the empire's territories and trade, overseeing the collection of taxes and ensuring the security of the trade routes.

While the Ghana Empire's power and wealth were centered in the north, its influence extended into Ivory Coast and other neighboring regions. Ivory Coast served as a conduit for the trade of gold and ivory from the empire's interior to the coast, where it would be exchanged with Arab and European traders for a wide range of commodities.

The decline of the Ghana Empire in the 11th century marked the end of an era, but its legacy lived on in the form of trade networks and cultural influences that continued to shape the Ivory Coast and the broader West African region. The empire's enduring impact on the history and prosperity of Ivory Coast is a testament to the enduring significance of this ancient African powerhouse.

Songhai Influence: The Rise of Ivory Coast

The rise of Ivory Coast as a prominent region in West Africa's historical tapestry was profoundly influenced by the power and reach of the Songhai Empire. Emerging in the 15th century, the Songhai Empire's expansion and cultural influence left an indelible mark on Ivory Coast's history, shaping its political dynamics, trade networks, and cultural identity.

The Songhai Empire, which reached its zenith in the 16th century, was one of the largest and most powerful empires in African history. It was situated in what is now Mali, Niger, and parts of Ivory Coast, and it controlled vast territories encompassing diverse ethnic groups and cultures.

One of the most significant aspects of the Songhai Empire's influence on Ivory Coast was its control over trade routes. The empire's strategic location allowed it to dominate trade routes that extended deep into the West African interior, facilitating the exchange of goods such as gold, salt, textiles, and, notably, ivory.

Ivory Coast's proximity to the Songhai Empire meant that it played a pivotal role in these trade networks. Ivory, derived from the abundant elephant populations of the region, was a highly sought-after commodity. It flowed through the Songhai-controlled trade routes, making its way to North African and European markets.

In addition to facilitating the trade of ivory, Ivory Coast

also served as a gateway for the spread of cultural and religious influences from the Songhai Empire. Islam, which was a dominant faith in the Songhai Empire, found its way into Ivory Coast through these trade routes. As merchants and travelers traversed the region, they brought with them Islamic beliefs, practices, and institutions.

The cultural exchanges that occurred as a result of these interactions enriched Ivory Coast's cultural mosaic. The blending of indigenous traditions with Islamic influences gave rise to unique syncretic practices and artistic expressions. Notably, Ivory Coast's wooden masks, sculptures, and textiles began to exhibit a fusion of local and Islamic motifs, reflecting the dynamic nature of cultural exchange.

Politically, the influence of the Songhai Empire was felt in Ivory Coast as well. The empire's administrative systems, including its use of regional governors and tax collection mechanisms, influenced the governance structures in parts of Ivory Coast. While the region remained politically diverse, the legacy of the Songhai Empire's administrative practices endured.

It is important to note that while the Songhai Empire's influence on Ivory Coast was significant, the region maintained a degree of autonomy and continued to be home to various ethnic groups and chiefdoms with their own distinct identities. However, the interactions with the Songhai Empire played a pivotal role in shaping the historical trajectory of Ivory Coast.

The decline of the Songhai Empire in the late 16th century marked a period of political and cultural transformation in Ivory Coast. The vacuum left by the Songhai's weakening authority allowed for the rise of new kingdoms and empires in the region, each contributing to the rich mosaic of Ivory Coast's history.

The Songhai Empire's influence on Ivory Coast was a crucial chapter in the region's story, impacting its trade, culture, and political landscape. As Ivory Coast continued to evolve and adapt to changing circumstances, it drew from the lessons and legacies of its encounters with the Songhai Empire, further enriching its own historical narrative.

Trans-Saharan Trade Routes: Ivory Coast's Role

The story of Ivory Coast's historical significance would be incomplete without an exploration of its pivotal role in the vast and intricate web of trans-Saharan trade routes. These trade routes, which connected West Africa to North Africa and beyond, were instrumental in shaping the region's destiny, fostering cultural exchanges, and driving economic prosperity.

Trans-Saharan trade was the lifeline of the ancient world, and Ivory Coast occupied a strategic position within this network. Situated along the Gulf of Guinea, Ivory Coast was not only a rich source of valuable commodities but also a crucial intermediary between the West African interior and the Mediterranean world.

The trans-Saharan trade routes were characterized by a complex network of caravans that traversed the arid Sahara Desert. These caravans carried a wide array of goods, including gold, ivory, salt, spices, textiles, and precious metals. Ivory Coast, with its abundance of ivory and gold, was a sought-after destination along these routes.

One of the most significant commodities traded along the trans-Saharan routes was, as the name suggests, salt. This essential mineral was mined in the Sahara and transported southward to be exchanged for gold, ivory, and other valuable resources. The exchange of salt for gold was a fundamental aspect of this trade, and Ivory Coast contributed to this economic exchange.

Gold, another coveted resource, was one of Ivory Coast's most valuable exports. The region's gold mines, hidden in its forests and riverbanks, attracted the attention of traders from across the Sahara. Caravans laden with gold dust and nuggets made their way northward, ultimately reaching North African and European markets.

Ivory, however, was perhaps the most iconic commodity traded along these routes. Ivory Coast's lush landscapes were home to a thriving elephant population, and the ivory tusks harvested from these animals were highly sought after for their beauty and utility. The ivory trade played a central role in Ivory Coast's interactions with North African and European traders.

As Ivory Coast became integrated into the trans-Saharan trade network, it also became a melting pot of cultures and ideas. Merchants, travelers, and scholars from North Africa brought with them Islamic beliefs, practices, and institutions. This Islamic influence gradually took root in the region, contributing to its cultural and religious diversity.

The trans-Saharan trade routes also facilitated the exchange of artistic and cultural expressions. Ivory Coast's indigenous craftsmanship, particularly in the creation of intricate wooden masks, sculptures, and textiles, gained recognition and demand in the wider marketplace. These works of art bore witness to the fusion of local traditions with foreign influences.

Ivory Coast's role in the trans-Saharan trade routes not only contributed to its economic prosperity but also left a lasting impact on its cultural identity. The trade networks that crisscrossed the region connected it to the broader world, enriching its historical tapestry with a tapestry of influences and legacies.

While the trans-Saharan trade routes were instrumental in Ivory Coast's history, they were not without challenges. The arduous journey through the Sahara Desert was fraught with dangers, and caravans had to navigate hostile environments and face threats from desert nomads and bandits.

The decline of the trans-Saharan trade routes in the 16th century, due in part to the opening of maritime trade routes and shifts in global trade patterns, marked a new chapter in Ivory Coast's history. Yet, the legacy of these ancient trade networks endures, reminding us of the region's pivotal role in connecting Africa to the world and shaping its cultural and economic evolution.

The Arrival of Islam: Faith and Culture

The arrival of Islam in Ivory Coast was a transformative chapter in its history, influencing not only the religious landscape but also leaving an indelible mark on its culture, society, and way of life. The spread of Islam in the region was a complex and multifaceted process, spanning centuries and characterized by a blending of indigenous traditions with the new faith.

The earliest traces of Islam's presence in Ivory Coast can be traced back to the 11th century, a testament to the faith's gradual spread through trade networks. Arab traders, primarily from North Africa, played a pivotal role in introducing Islam to the region. They arrived along the coast and, through interactions with local communities, began to disseminate Islamic beliefs and practices.

Trade was the conduit through which Islam made its inroads into Ivory Coast. The trans-Saharan trade routes, which passed through the region, facilitated contact between North African Muslim merchants and indigenous peoples. This interaction led to the exchange of not only goods but also ideas and religious beliefs.

Islam's appeal was multifaceted. For some, it offered a spiritual path, promising salvation and a deeper understanding of the divine. For others, it provided access to the networks and opportunities of the wider Islamic world, including trade and scholarship. Over time, Islamic communities and mosques began to take root in Ivory

Coast, becoming centers of religious and cultural life.

One of the most significant aspects of Islam's influence was the spread of the Arabic script and language. Arabic became the language of religion and scholarship, with Islamic schools, or madrasas, teaching Arabic alongside religious texts. This linguistic shift had a profound impact on Ivory Coast's cultural and intellectual development.

As Islam gained a foothold in Ivory Coast, it intersected with indigenous traditions and belief systems. This syncretic blending of Islamic and traditional practices gave rise to unique cultural expressions and rituals. Local traditions, such as ancestor worship and animistic beliefs, coexisted with Islamic religious practices, creating a rich tapestry of religious diversity.

The spread of Islam also influenced Ivory Coast's social structures and governance. Islamic law, or Sharia, began to play a role in adjudicating disputes and maintaining order within Muslim communities. Some rulers and elites converted to Islam, aligning themselves with the faith's authority and institutions.

One of the most enduring legacies of Islam's arrival was the architecture of mosques and religious structures. These buildings showcased intricate designs and artistic motifs, reflecting the fusion of Islamic and local artistic traditions. The Great Mosque of Kong, for instance, exemplifies this architectural blend, with its distinctive Sahelian style.

The practice of Islamic rituals, such as prayer and fasting during Ramadan, became integral to the daily lives of Ivory Coast's Muslim communities. The faith also contributed to a sense of identity and belonging, providing a unifying force among diverse ethnic groups.

It's important to note that while Islam had a significant impact, Ivory Coast remained a religiously diverse nation. Indigenous beliefs and Christianity also coexisted alongside Islam, creating a pluralistic religious landscape.

In conclusion, the arrival of Islam in Ivory Coast was a multifaceted and transformative process that unfolded over centuries. It influenced not only religious practices but also language, culture, and social structures, shaping the region's identity as a diverse and dynamic society where Islam played a pivotal role in its cultural and historical evolution.

Kingdoms Along the Coast: The Akan and Baulé

The coastal regions of Ivory Coast, particularly in the south, have a rich history characterized by the presence of distinct ethnic groups and the emergence of powerful kingdoms. Among the most notable of these groups are the Akan and Baulé, whose histories are intertwined with the cultural, political, and social fabric of Ivory Coast's coastal regions.

The Akan people are a prominent ethnic group in Ivory Coast, and they have a long and storied history in the region. The Akan are known for their intricate artistry, vibrant traditions, and complex social structures. Their presence in Ivory Coast dates back centuries, and their influence can still be seen and felt in the region today.

One of the most significant Akan kingdoms was the Ashanti Empire, which extended from what is now Ghana into parts of Ivory Coast. The Ashanti Empire was a powerful and well-organized state known for its military prowess, artistic achievements, and complex administrative systems. While the heart of the Ashanti Empire lay to the west of Ivory Coast, its influence reached into the southwestern regions of the country.

The Akan people, including those within the Ashanti Empire, have a rich artistic heritage. They are renowned for their craftsmanship in various forms, such as woodcarving, beadwork, and textiles. These artistic traditions are not only decorative but also carry deep cultural and spiritual significance, often used in rituals, ceremonies, and as symbols of identity.

The Baulé, another important ethnic group in Ivory Coast, are known for their unique cultural practices and artistic expressions. The Baulé are famous for their intricately carved wooden masks, which play a central role in their religious and cultural traditions. These masks are used in various ceremonies and rituals, representing ancestral spirits and cultural stories.

One of the defining features of Baulé society is its strong emphasis on the concept of "gbekre." Gbekre encompasses the Baulé belief in the supernatural, ancestral guidance, and the connection between the living and the dead. Gbekre ceremonies involve the use of masks and dances to invoke ancestral spirits and seek their guidance and protection.

The Akan and Baulé people, like other ethnic groups in Ivory Coast, have historically organized themselves into chiefdoms and kingdoms. These political structures played a crucial role in governance, justice, and the administration of local affairs. Chiefs, or leaders, held significant authority within their respective communities.

The coastal regions inhabited by the Akan and Baulé peoples were also significant in Ivory Coast's trade networks. The proximity to the coast made these regions vital hubs for the exchange of goods, both regionally and with foreign traders. This trade contributed to the economic prosperity and cultural diversity of the coastal areas.

The arrival of European colonizers in the late 19th century and the subsequent colonization of Ivory Coast marked a significant turning point in the history of the Akan and

Baulé peoples. Colonial rule brought about changes in governance, landownership, and economic systems, leading to shifts in traditional societies.

Despite the challenges of colonialism and later political developments, the Akan and Baulé cultures have endured and continue to play a vital role in Ivory Coast's cultural landscape. Their artistic traditions, spiritual beliefs, and social structures remain integral to the country's identity and serve as a testament to the resilience and vitality of these coastal kingdoms.

The Portuguese Connection: European Exploration

The arrival of European explorers in the coastal regions of what is now Ivory Coast marked a new chapter in the country's history. Among the earliest European powers to establish a presence in the region were the Portuguese, whose exploration and interactions with the local populations laid the groundwork for subsequent European colonialism.

The Portuguese explorers were among the first Europeans to venture into the waters of the Gulf of Guinea and along the coast of present-day Ivory Coast. Their initial forays were driven by a quest for new trade routes, valuable resources, and potential markets. Ivory Coast, with its abundant ivory, gold, and spices, held great allure for these explorers.

The late 15th century witnessed the emergence of Portuguese maritime exploration along the West African coast. Navigators like Diogo Cão and Alvise Cadamosto made significant voyages, mapping the coastline and establishing contact with local African communities. These early interactions laid the foundation for trade and cultural exchange.

Ivory Coast's coastal regions, particularly the areas around present-day Grand-Bassam and Assinie, became focal points for Portuguese trade and exploration. The Portuguese established trading posts and forts along the coast, including São Jorge da Mina (now Elmina) in modern Ghana. These forts served as bases for conducting trade and establishing European influence in the region.

One of the primary commodities that attracted the Portuguese to Ivory Coast was, as the name suggests, ivory. The lush forests and savannas of the region were home to an abundant population of elephants, making it a key source of ivory tusks. These tusks were highly valued in European markets for their ornamental and practical uses.

Gold, another precious resource, was also a major incentive for Portuguese explorers. Ivory Coast's gold mines, concealed in its interior, yielded a steady supply of this coveted metal. Gold was a symbol of wealth and power and played a central role in European efforts to exploit the region's resources.

The Portuguese presence in Ivory Coast brought about cultural exchanges and interactions between European explorers and local populations. European goods, including textiles, ceramics, and firearms, made their way into the region through trade. In return, Ivory Coast exported its valuable commodities, including ivory, gold, and kola nuts.

It's important to note that the arrival of European explorers also had significant consequences for the local populations. While trade brought material benefits, it also introduced new diseases and vulnerabilities. The disruption caused by European expansion would set the stage for more profound changes in Ivory Coast's history, including later colonization by European powers.

The Portuguese influence along the Ivory Coast coast was not enduring. By the early 16th century, other European powers, including the Dutch, French, and English, began to challenge Portuguese dominance in the region. These competing interests and conflicts would ultimately reshape the geopolitical landscape of Ivory Coast.

In retrospect, the Portuguese connection in Ivory Coast's history serves as a prologue to the broader European exploration and colonization of the region. It laid the groundwork for the complex interactions, cultural exchanges, and power struggles that would come to define Ivory Coast's history in the centuries to follow.

The Era of Slavery: Impact on Ivory Coast

The era of slavery stands as a dark chapter in the history of Ivory Coast, as it does for much of Africa. This period, which spanned several centuries, had profound and enduring effects on the region, reshaping its demographics, societies, and economies.

The Atlantic slave trade, which began in the 16th century, marked a significant turning point in Ivory Coast's history. European powers, including the Portuguese, Dutch, French, and English, established trading posts along the coast to facilitate the capture, purchase, and transportation of enslaved Africans to the Americas.

Ivory Coast's coastal regions, with their access to the Atlantic Ocean, became important hubs in the transatlantic slave trade. European traders established fortified trading posts and forts along the coast, from which they conducted the brutal business of capturing and enslaving Africans.

The impact of the transatlantic slave trade on Ivory Coast was multifaceted. One of the most devastating consequences was the loss of countless lives. African men, women, and children were forcibly taken from their communities, families torn apart, and subjected to inhumane conditions during their journey across the Atlantic.

The demographic impact of the slave trade on Ivory Coast was significant. Entire communities were decimated, and some regions saw a sharp decline in their populations. The labor force, essential for agricultural and economic activities, was disrupted, leading to economic instability and social upheaval.

While the majority of enslaved Africans from Ivory Coast were transported to the Americas, a significant number were retained for forced labor within the region. Plantations and trading posts in Ivory Coast relied on enslaved labor to produce goods for the transatlantic trade, including products like ivory, gold, and kola nuts.

The effects of the transatlantic slave trade extended beyond the economic realm. It disrupted social structures and traditional ways of life. Communities that were heavily impacted by the trade often experienced cultural disintegration, as the loss of key members and social disruptions eroded their cultural practices and institutions.

The transatlantic slave trade also left a lasting legacy of trauma and collective memory. Oral histories and traditions passed down through generations bear witness to the suffering endured by those who were enslaved and their descendants. This historical trauma continues to influence the cultural consciousness of Ivory Coast and the broader African diaspora.

The eventual abolition of the transatlantic slave trade in the 19th century did not immediately alleviate the suffering of those who had been enslaved or their descendants. Many faced ongoing discrimination and economic hardship, as the scars of slavery lingered in Ivory Coast and beyond.

It is important to acknowledge that the era of slavery was not solely defined by victimhood. African resistance to slavery was a powerful and enduring force. Enslaved Africans and their communities resisted captivity through various means, including acts of rebellion, escape, and the preservation of cultural and spiritual traditions.

The legacy of slavery remains a complex and deeply ingrained part of Ivory Coast's history. It serves as a reminder of the enduring impact of historical injustices and the resilience of African peoples in the face of adversity. The story of slavery in Ivory Coast, like elsewhere, is a testament to the strength and resilience of those who endured its horrors.

Colonial Ambitions: France's Arrival

The late 19th century witnessed the intensification of European colonial ambitions across Africa, and Ivory Coast was not immune to the wave of imperialistic fervor that swept the continent. France, as one of the major colonial powers, set its sights on Ivory Coast, a region abundant in resources and strategic importance.

The French colonial venture in Ivory Coast was driven by multifaceted ambitions. Economic interests were paramount, as the region held vast reserves of valuable resources, including timber, palm oil, cocoa, coffee, and rubber. Ivory Coast's fertile lands also offered agricultural potential that could be harnessed for the benefit of the French economy.

The Ivory Coast region was particularly coveted for its production of commodities that were in high demand globally. Cocoa, in particular, would become a cornerstone of the colonial economy. French colonial administrators recognized the profitability of cocoa cultivation and established plantations, often relying on forced labor to maximize production.

The French colonial presence in Ivory Coast was initially met with resistance from local communities. Several indigenous groups, including the Baoulé and Bété, resisted French encroachment on their lands and attempted to defend their autonomy and way of life. However, the superior military technology and firepower of the French forces often tipped the scales in their favor.

The French colonial administration imposed a new order on Ivory Coast. It introduced administrative structures, taxation systems, and legal frameworks that served the interests of the colonial power. Land was expropriated from local communities, often resulting in the displacement of indigenous peoples from their ancestral territories.

One of the most significant developments during the colonial era was the construction of a vast network of infrastructure, including roads, railways, and ports. These infrastructure projects aimed to facilitate the extraction of Ivory Coast's resources and their transportation to European markets. They also facilitated the movement of labor between different regions of Ivory Coast.

Labor was a central issue during the colonial period. Forced labor was widespread on plantations and in various sectors of the economy, and it was used to fuel the colonial economic machine. African laborers were subjected to harsh working conditions, and many were forced to leave their communities and homes to toil on plantations and in mines.

The colonial administration also played a role in reshaping the cultural and social fabric of Ivory Coast. French language and culture were promoted, and indigenous languages and traditions were marginalized. Christianity, particularly Catholicism, was actively promoted by French missionaries, leading to the conversion of many Ivorians to the faith.

The impact of French colonialism on Ivory Coast was profound and enduring. It left a legacy of economic exploitation, cultural transformation, and social disruption. The forced labor system, which persisted well into the 20th century, left scars on the collective memory of Ivory Coast's population.

The drive for independence from colonial rule began to gain momentum in the mid-20th century, and Ivory Coast would eventually achieve its independence from France in 1960. However, the legacy of colonialism, including its impact on landownership, social structures, and economic systems, continued to shape the nation's post-independence trajectory.

In retrospect, the era of French colonialism in Ivory Coast serves as a complex chapter in the nation's history, marked by exploitation and resistance, cultural transformation and continuity. It is a period that cannot be separated from Ivory Coast's journey toward nationhood and the challenges it would face in forging a new identity and future in the post-colonial era.

Scramble for Africa: Ivory Coast under French Rule

The late 19th century was a tumultuous period in Ivory Coast's history as it, like much of Africa, became embroiled in the Scramble for Africa—a frantic race among European powers to colonize and control vast swaths of the continent. In this frenzied contest, France emerged as a major player, and Ivory Coast found itself thrust into the orbit of the French colonial machine.

The Scramble for Africa was driven by a complex web of motivations. European powers sought to expand their territorial holdings, access valuable resources, and establish markets for their goods. In the case of France, Ivory Coast's strategic location along the West African coast and its wealth of resources made it an attractive prize.

France's interest in Ivory Coast grew as it sought to consolidate its influence in the region. French explorers and traders ventured into the Ivory Coast interior, mapping the land and establishing contact with indigenous communities. They were often met with resistance, as local populations sought to defend their autonomy and way of life against the encroaching European powers.

One of the defining moments in Ivory Coast's colonial history was the signing of the Treaty of Grand-Bassam in 1887. This treaty established French control over Ivory Coast's coastal regions and set the stage for further expansion into the interior. French colonial administrators established a series of forts and trading posts along the coast, solidifying their presence.

The penetration of French influence into Ivory Coast's interior was facilitated by superior military technology and firepower. Indigenous resistance, while formidable, often succumbed to the overwhelming might of French forces. This paved the way for the expansion of French control over larger portions of the territory.

The colonial administration imposed its authority through a system of governance that served the interests of the colonial power. Ivory Coast was incorporated into French West Africa as a colony and later as part of the French Union. Administrative structures, taxation systems, and legal frameworks were established to extract resources and labor for the benefit of France.

Landownership underwent a significant transformation during the colonial period. Land was expropriated from local communities, often without their consent, and placed under the control of the colonial administration or European settlers. This resulted in the displacement of indigenous peoples from their ancestral lands.

Economically, Ivory Coast became an integral part of the French colonial economic system. The region's abundant resources, including cocoa, coffee, rubber, and timber, were exploited for the profit of the colonial power. Forced labor was widespread, with African laborers toiling on plantations and in mines under harsh conditions.

Infrastructure development was another hallmark of the French colonial era. Roads, railways, and ports were constructed to facilitate the extraction of Ivory Coast's resources and their transportation to European markets.

These infrastructure projects also facilitated the movement of labor between different regions of Ivory Coast.

The colonial administration actively promoted French language and culture, while indigenous languages and traditions were marginalized. Christianity, particularly Catholicism, was actively promoted by French missionaries, leading to the conversion of many Ivorians to the faith. These cultural transformations had a lasting impact on Ivory Coast's society.

The impact of French colonialism on Ivory Coast was profound and enduring. It left a legacy of economic exploitation, cultural transformation, and social disruption. The forced labor system, which persisted well into the 20th century, left scars on the collective memory of Ivory Coast's population.

In retrospect, the era of French colonialism in Ivory Coast serves as a complex chapter in the nation's history, marked by exploitation and resistance, cultural transformation and continuity. It is a period that cannot be separated from Ivory Coast's journey toward nationhood and the challenges it would face in forging a new identity and future in the post-colonial era.

Plantations and Labor: The Colonial Economy

The colonial economy that emerged during Ivory Coast's period of French colonial rule was intricately woven into the fabric of global trade and exploitation. At the heart of this colonial economic system were plantations and forced labor, which formed the backbone of Ivory Coast's contribution to the global market.

The French colonial administration, driven by the desire to extract maximum economic value from Ivory Coast's abundant resources, established large-scale plantations across the territory. These plantations focused on the cultivation of cash crops, most notably cocoa, coffee, rubber, and oil palm.

Cocoa emerged as the crown jewel of Ivory Coast's colonial economy. The region's favorable climate and fertile soil made it an ideal location for cocoa cultivation. French colonial administrators and European settlers established cocoa plantations throughout the territory, transforming Ivory Coast into a leading global producer of cocoa.

Coffee, while not as dominant as cocoa, also played a significant role in Ivory Coast's colonial economy. Coffee plantations dotted the landscape, particularly in the western regions. Rubber and oil palm plantations, too, contributed to the diversity of cash crops cultivated in the colony.

The success of these plantations hinged on the availability

of labor, and the French colonial administration employed various coercive tactics to secure a workforce. Forced labor became a cornerstone of the colonial economic system. African laborers, often subjected to brutal working conditions, were conscripted to toil on plantations and in mines.

The forced labor system was not confined to plantations; it extended to various sectors of the colonial economy. Laborers were subjected to grueling work, from clearing land and planting crops to harvesting and processing raw materials. The forced labor system was marked by exploitation, abuse, and the disruption of traditional ways of life.

The consequences of forced labor reverberated throughout Ivory Coast's society. Families were separated as men and women were conscripted to work in different regions. Entire communities were uprooted, their cultural and social fabric torn apart by the demands of the colonial economy.

French colonial administrators introduced a system of taxation that further burdened the labor force. Taxes were levied on the production of cash crops, further incentivizing labor on plantations. The combination of forced labor and taxation left many Ivorians trapped in cycles of debt and dependency.

The exploitation of Ivory Coast's resources did not benefit the local population. The profits from cash crops flowed to French and European companies and colonial authorities. The unequal distribution of wealth and resources exacerbated social and economic disparities within the colony.

Infrastructure development, such as roads and railways, played a dual role in the colonial economy. While these projects facilitated the extraction of resources, they also contributed to the displacement of local communities. Land was expropriated to make way for infrastructure projects, further marginalizing indigenous populations.

The colonial economic system was intricately linked to global markets. Ivory Coast's cash crops, particularly cocoa and coffee, were in high demand internationally. French and European companies profited from Ivory Coast's production, while the Ivorian labor force bore the brunt of the exploitation.

In summary, the colonial economy that thrived during Ivory Coast's period of French colonial rule was built on the twin pillars of plantations and forced labor. This economic system, driven by the pursuit of profit, left lasting scars on Ivory Coast's society and contributed to the economic disparities that persisted into the post-colonial era. It is a stark reminder of the complex legacies of colonialism in the nation's history.

From Ivory Coast to Côte d'Ivoire: A Nation Emerges

The journey from Ivory Coast to Côte d'Ivoire represents a critical chapter in the nation's history, marked by the transition from colonial rule to independence and the forging of a new national identity. This transformation was characterized by challenges, opportunities, and a quest for self-determination.

The struggle for independence from French colonial rule gained momentum in the mid-20th century, as Ivory Coast, like other African nations, sought to break free from the shackles of foreign domination. The winds of change were blowing across the African continent, and nationalist movements began to gain strength.

Ivory Coast's path to independence was marked by both peaceful negotiations and confrontations. Félix Houphouët-Boigny, a prominent Ivorian leader, played a central role in the nation's transition to self-rule. He pursued a moderate approach, advocating for gradual self-government and cooperation with the French administration.

In 1958, Ivory Coast voted in a referendum to remain within the French Community, albeit with increased autonomy. This decision was influenced by the belief that cooperation with France would be beneficial in ensuring a stable and prosperous future for the newly emerging nation.

On August 7, 1960, Ivory Coast officially achieved independence from France and became a sovereign nation.

This historic moment marked the culmination of years of negotiations, political maneuvering, and a desire for self-determination. Ivory Coast joined the community of newly independent African nations, taking its place on the global stage.

Félix Houphouët-Boigny, who had been a key figure in the nation's transition to independence, became Ivory Coast's first president and would go on to lead the country for several decades. His leadership, characterized by a commitment to stability and economic development, shaped Ivory Coast's early years as an independent nation.

One of the central challenges faced by the new nation was the task of nation-building. Ivory Coast was a diverse country with a mosaic of ethnic groups, languages, and cultural traditions. The government sought to foster a sense of national unity and identity while respecting the diversity of its population.

Economically, Ivory Coast embarked on a path of development and modernization. The country's abundant resources, including cocoa, coffee, and timber, were harnessed to drive economic growth. Infrastructure projects, such as roads and ports, were initiated to facilitate trade and transport.

Ivory Coast's cocoa production, in particular, played a pivotal role in its economic development. The nation became one of the world's leading producers of cocoa, and the crop played a significant role in generating revenue and driving economic growth.

Despite the optimism of the early post-independence years, Ivory Coast faced its share of challenges. Political stability was periodically tested, and the nation experienced periods of civil unrest and political strife. Ethnic tensions and competition for resources sometimes flared into violence.

The 1990s were a particularly turbulent period in Ivory Coast's history, marked by political upheaval and armed conflict. The nation grappled with issues related to governance, identity, and citizenship. The division between the north and south, exacerbated by political and ethnic factors, deepened during this time.

Efforts to reconcile and reunify the nation continued into the 21st century. A peace agreement was brokered in 2007, leading to a period of relative stability and the eventual disarmament of rebel forces. Ivory Coast began the process of healing and rebuilding.

Ivory Coast officially changed its name to Côte d'Ivoire in 1985, reflecting the government's desire to emphasize its African identity and cultural heritage. The name change was intended to promote a sense of national pride and unity.

The 21st century brought both opportunities and challenges for Côte d'Ivoire. The nation's economy continued to grow, and efforts were made to address social and development issues. However, political tensions and electoral disputes remained a part of the national landscape.

In 2010, Côte d'Ivoire faced a significant political crisis following a disputed presidential election. The crisis escalated into violence, raising concerns about the nation's stability and future. International intervention, along with diplomatic efforts, ultimately helped resolve the crisis and restore calm.

Côte d'Ivoire continues to grapple with the complex task of nation-building, reconciliation, and political stability. The nation's journey from Ivory Coast to Côte d'Ivoire reflects the enduring quest for self-determination and the challenges inherent in forging a cohesive and prosperous nation. It is a story of resilience, diversity, and the ongoing pursuit of a brighter future.

Nationalism and Independence: The Mid-20th Century

The mid-20th century marked a transformative period in the history of Côte d'Ivoire, as the nation, like many others across Africa, embarked on a journey toward independence and self-determination. This era was defined by the rise of nationalism, the struggle against colonial rule, and the aspiration for autonomy.

Nationalism, the fervent belief in and promotion of one's nation's interests and culture, became a powerful force in Côte d'Ivoire during the mid-20th century. The seeds of nationalism had been sown through years of colonial rule, as Ivorians began to question the legitimacy and impact of French colonialism on their land and lives.

African leaders and intellectuals played a central role in nurturing the flames of nationalism. Figures like Félix Houphouët-Boigny emerged as key figures in the nationalist movement. They advocated for Ivorian autonomy and the end of colonial rule, recognizing that true self-determination could only be achieved through independence.

The struggle for independence in Côte d'Ivoire was not without its challenges and complexities. The nation's journey toward self-rule was characterized by a combination of peaceful negotiations, political activism, and, at times, confrontations with the colonial administration.

In 1958, a pivotal moment arrived when Côte d'Ivoire, alongside other French African colonies, was asked to vote in a referendum on its political future. Ivorians were presented with two options: to remain within the French Community with increased autonomy or to choose full independence. The majority of Ivorians voted to remain within the French Community but with greater self-governing powers.

This choice, often referred to as the "No" vote, was influenced by various factors. Many Ivorians believed that cooperation with France would provide a more stable and prosperous path toward self-rule. Félix Houphouët-Boigny and other leaders believed in a gradual approach to independence, seeking to maintain stability during the transition.

The path to independence was not straightforward, and negotiations with the French government were a key element of the process. These negotiations culminated in the attainment of full independence for Côte d'Ivoire on August 7, 1960. It was a historic moment that marked the nation's emergence as a sovereign state.

Félix Houphouët-Boigny, who had played a central role in the nation's journey toward independence, became Côte d'Ivoire's first president. His leadership, characterized by a commitment to stability and economic development, would shape the nation's early years as an independent nation.

One of the central challenges faced by the new nation was nation-building. Côte d'Ivoire was a diverse country with a mosaic of ethnic groups, languages, and cultural traditions. The government sought to foster a sense of national unity and identity while respecting the diversity of its population.

Economically, Côte d'Ivoire embarked on a path of development and modernization. The country's abundant resources, including cocoa, coffee, and timber, were harnessed to drive economic growth. Infrastructure projects, such as roads and ports, were initiated to facilitate trade and transport.

Côte d'Ivoire's cocoa production, in particular, played a pivotal role in its economic development. The nation became one of the world's leading producers of cocoa, and the crop played a significant role in generating revenue and driving economic growth.

Despite the optimism of the early post-independence years, Côte d'Ivoire faced its share of challenges. Political stability was periodically tested, and the nation experienced periods of civil unrest and political strife. Ethnic tensions and competition for resources sometimes flared into violence.

The 1990s were a particularly turbulent period in Côte d'Ivoire's history, marked by political upheaval and armed conflict. The nation grappled with issues related to governance, identity, and citizenship. The division between the north and south, exacerbated by political and ethnic factors, deepened during this time.

Efforts to reconcile and reunify the nation continued into the 21st century. A peace agreement was brokered in 2007, leading to a period of relative stability and the eventual disarmament of rebel forces. Côte d'Ivoire began the process of healing and rebuilding.

In summary, the mid-20th century was a pivotal era in Côte d'Ivoire's history, defined by the rise of nationalism, the struggle for independence, and the nation's emergence as a sovereign state. It was a period marked by both optimism and challenges, and it laid the foundation for the complex and evolving story of modern Côte d'Ivoire.

Félix Houphouët-Boigny: Founding Father and Leader

Félix Houphouët-Boigny, a towering figure in the history of Côte d'Ivoire, emerged as a key architect of the nation's journey from colonialism to independence and its subsequent development as a sovereign state. His leadership and vision left an indelible mark on the trajectory of Côte d'Ivoire, earning him the distinction of being the nation's founding father and its first president.

Born on October 18, 1905, in Yamoussoukro, Félix Houphouët-Boigny was raised in a region that would later become the political and symbolic heart of Côte d'Ivoire. He was the son of a Baoulé chief, which provided him with a privileged upbringing and an early exposure to the dynamics of local leadership and governance.

Houphouët-Boigny's educational journey was marked by ambition and determination. He pursued his studies in Dakar, Senegal, and later in France, where he obtained a medical degree in 1935. His medical training would serve as the foundation of his early career, but his passion for politics and the welfare of his people would ultimately shape his destiny.

Returning to Côte d'Ivoire in the 1930s, Houphouët-Boigny embarked on a multifaceted career. He continued to practice medicine, addressing the healthcare needs of his fellow Ivorians, but his political aspirations were evident. He became involved in the nascent political movements advocating for Ivorian autonomy.

One of his notable achievements during this period was the founding of the Syndicat Agricole Africain, an organization dedicated to representing the interests of African farmers. This marked the beginning of his advocacy for the rights and welfare of rural communities, a cause that would remain close to his heart throughout his political career.

The rise of Félix Houphouët-Boigny as a political leader gained momentum during the tumultuous years of World War II and the post-war period. He seized the opportunity to engage with French authorities and advocate for increased autonomy for Côte d'Ivoire. His diplomatic skills and ability to build relationships with key figures in France played a pivotal role in advancing the cause of Ivorian self-determination.

Houphouët-Boigny's moderate and pragmatic approach to achieving independence set him apart as a leader. He recognized the importance of gradual transition and cooperation with the French administration. This approach culminated in the 1958 referendum, where Ivorians voted to remain within the French Community but with greater self-governing powers.

After Côte d'Ivoire achieved independence on August 7, 1960, Félix Houphouët-Boigny assumed the role of the nation's first president. His leadership style was characterized by a commitment to stability, economic development, and social harmony. He espoused a philosophy known as "Ivorian Socialism," which emphasized a balance between state intervention in the economy and private enterprise.

Under his leadership, Côte d'Ivoire experienced significant economic growth. The nation's abundant resources, particularly cocoa, coffee, and timber, were harnessed to drive economic development. Infrastructure projects, including roads, ports, and educational institutions, were initiated to modernize the nation and improve the quality of life for its citizens.

Côte d'Ivoire's cocoa production, in particular, became a cornerstone of its economy. Houphouët-Boigny's policies incentivized cocoa cultivation, making Côte d'Ivoire one of the world's leading producers of the crop. The revenues generated from cocoa exports played a crucial role in financing the nation's development initiatives.

Houphouët-Boigny's leadership extended beyond his domestic achievements. He played a prominent role in regional and international diplomacy, advocating for African unity and cooperation. He was a proponent of the idea of "African personality," which emphasized the unique character of African nations and their right to shape their destinies. Despite the achievements of his presidency, Houphouët-Boigny's rule was not without controversy. His leadership style was characterized by a strong central government, and he maintained a one-party rule for much of his time in office. This led to criticism of his commitment to democracy and political pluralism.

Félix Houphouët-Boigny's leadership came to an end with his passing on December 7, 1993. His death marked the end of an era in Côte d'Ivoire's history, but his legacy endured. He left behind a nation that had made significant strides in economic development and infrastructure, as well as a political landscape shaped by his influence.

In retrospect, Félix Houphouët-Boigny's legacy is a complex and multifaceted one. He is celebrated as the founding father of Côte d'Ivoire and a visionary leader who played a pivotal role in the nation's journey to independence and development. His leadership, though at times controversial, remains a defining chapter in the nation's history, shaping its identity and trajectory on the African continent.

The Politics of Stability: One-Party Rule

One of the defining features of Côte d'Ivoire's post-independence political landscape was the predominance of one-party rule under the leadership of Félix Houphouët-Boigny. This era, often characterized by political stability, economic development, and a unique approach to governance, left a lasting impact on the nation's trajectory.

Upon assuming the presidency in 1960, Félix Houphouët-Boigny and his party, the Democratic Party of Côte d'Ivoire (PDCI), established a firm grip on political power. The PDCI became the dominant political force in the country, and its leader maintained a central role in shaping the nation's policies and direction.

Houphouët-Boigny's approach to governance was grounded in his belief in the importance of stability and social harmony. He sought to foster a sense of national unity and cohesion among the diverse ethnic and cultural groups that comprised Côte d'Ivoire. To achieve this, he emphasized a brand of politics that transcended ethnic and regional divisions.

One-party rule was a central element of Houphouët-Boigny's political philosophy. The PDCI was the sole legal political party in Côte d'Ivoire for much of his presidency. This one-party system allowed for centralized decision-making and provided a degree of political stability that was uncommon in many other African nations during the post-independence period.

Under Houphouët-Boigny's leadership, Côte d'Ivoire experienced significant economic growth and development. The nation's abundant resources, including cocoa, coffee, and timber, were harnessed to drive economic progress. Infrastructure projects, such as roads, ports, and educational institutions, were initiated to modernize the country and improve the quality of life for its citizens.

Côte d'Ivoire's cocoa production, in particular, became a cornerstone of its economy. Houphouët-Boigny's policies incentivized cocoa cultivation, making Côte d'Ivoire one of the world's leading producers of the crop. The revenues generated from cocoa exports played a crucial role in financing the nation's development initiatives.

The political stability and economic growth achieved under one-party rule earned Côte d'Ivoire a reputation as an oasis of peace and prosperity in a region often plagued by political turmoil and conflict. Houphouët-Boigny's leadership was lauded for its ability to maintain social cohesion and relative stability in the face of ethnic and regional diversity.

However, one-party rule also had its critics and detractors. While it provided a degree of stability, it limited political pluralism and the ability of opposition voices to be heard. The absence of competitive multiparty politics raised concerns about democracy and the openness of the political system.

Criticism of the one-party system grew over time, and calls for political reform and greater political openness began to mount. The 1990s witnessed a period of political change and transition, as pressure from civil society, opposition groups, and international actors led to the adoption of a new constitution in 2000 that allowed for multiparty elections.

The transition away from one-party rule marked a significant turning point in Côte d'Ivoire's political history. It signaled a shift toward a more pluralistic and competitive political landscape, although it also brought challenges, including electoral disputes and periods of political instability.

In summary, the politics of stability under one-party rule during Félix Houphouët-Boigny's presidency was a defining feature of Côte d'Ivoire's post-independence era. While it contributed to political stability and economic development, it also raised questions about democracy and political pluralism. The transition to a multiparty system in the late 1990s and early 2000s represented a fundamental shift in the nation's political landscape, reflecting the evolving aspirations of its citizens.

Cocoa and Coffee: Economic Pillars

Côte d'Ivoire's economic landscape has long been defined by the twin pillars of cocoa and coffee production. These cash crops have played a central role in shaping the nation's economy, driving growth, generating revenue, and contributing to the country's global prominence as a major producer of these commodities.

Cocoa, often referred to as "brown gold," stands out as one of Côte d'Ivoire's most crucial economic exports. The favorable climate and fertile soil of the country's southern regions make it an ideal location for cocoa cultivation. Côte d'Ivoire has consistently ranked as the world's largest producer of cocoa beans, accounting for a substantial portion of global cocoa production.

Cocoa cultivation in Côte d'Ivoire traces its roots to the colonial era when French colonial administrators and European settlers established cocoa plantations across the territory. This laid the foundation for the nation's cocoa industry, which would expand significantly in the post-independence period.

Under the leadership of President Félix Houphouët-Boigny, cocoa became a central component of Côte d'Ivoire's economic development strategy. The government implemented policies to incentivize cocoa farming, including providing subsidies, extension services, and access to credit for farmers. These measures aimed to increase cocoa production and improve the livelihoods of those engaged in its cultivation.

The results were remarkable. Côte d'Ivoire's cocoa production surged, and the nation's cocoa exports became a major source of revenue. The cocoa sector provided employment opportunities for a significant portion of the population, from small-scale farmers to laborers involved in cocoa processing and transportation.

While cocoa was the primary economic driver, coffee also played a significant role in Côte d'Ivoire's economy. Coffee plantations were established in various regions of the country, particularly in the west. Ivorian coffee, known for its quality, found its place in international markets, contributing to the nation's export earnings.

The cocoa and coffee sectors were characterized by both small-scale and large-scale production. Smallholder farmers cultivated cocoa and coffee on family-owned plots, while larger commercial plantations also existed. This diversity in production methods contributed to the resilience and sustainability of these industries.

Cocoa and coffee farming in Côte d'Ivoire was not without its challenges. The fluctuation of global commodity prices, disease outbreaks, and issues related to farm management presented ongoing concerns. Additionally, the environmental impact of cocoa and coffee cultivation, including deforestation, became subjects of scrutiny.

Efforts were made to address these challenges and promote sustainable farming practices. Initiatives focused on improving crop yields, reducing environmental impact, and ensuring fair prices for farmers were introduced. Côte d'Ivoire sought to balance the economic benefits of cocoa and coffee production with the need for environmental conservation and social responsibility.

The economic significance of cocoa and coffee in Côte d'Ivoire extended beyond agriculture. Processing industries, such as cocoa and coffee processing and chocolate manufacturing, also emerged, adding value to these commodities and creating additional employment opportunities.

The cocoa and coffee sectors remained central to Côte d'Ivoire's economy well into the 21st century. However, the nation's economic diversification efforts sought to reduce its reliance on these commodities and expand into other sectors, such as oil and gas, manufacturing, and services.

In conclusion, cocoa and coffee have been the economic pillars of Côte d'Ivoire, contributing significantly to the nation's economic growth and global reputation as a leading producer of these commodities. These industries have played a vital role in providing livelihoods for a substantial portion of the population and shaping the nation's economic landscape. As Côte d'Ivoire continues to evolve, its cocoa and coffee sectors remain emblematic of its economic prowess and agricultural heritage.

Challenges of Ethnic Diversity: National Unity

Côte d'Ivoire's ethnic diversity is both a source of richness and a challenge that has shaped the nation's history and politics. The country is home to over 60 distinct ethnic groups, each with its own languages, cultural traditions, and histories. This diversity, while contributing to the nation's cultural tapestry, has presented complex challenges in terms of forging national unity and identity.

The ethnic mosaic of Côte d'Ivoire can be broadly categorized into five main linguistic and cultural groups: the Akan, Krou, Mande, Gur, and other smaller ethnic communities. Among these, the Akan, which includes subgroups like the Baoulé and Bété, are the largest and have historically held significant influence.

The challenge of ethnic diversity is not unique to Côte d'Ivoire, but it has been particularly pronounced due to the nation's colonial history and post-independence politics. French colonial administrators often employed a policy of divide and rule, emphasizing ethnic and regional differences to maintain control. This strategy left a legacy of ethnic divisions that would persist into the post-independence era.

Côte d'Ivoire's first president, Félix Houphouët-Boigny, recognized the potential for ethnic tensions to undermine national unity. His leadership emphasized the importance of unity and sought to bridge ethnic divides. He promoted a vision of "Ivority," which emphasized the shared Ivorian identity over ethnic affiliations. However, the concept of "Ivority" would later become a source of controversy and division.

Ethnicity also became entwined with issues of citizenship and identity. In the 1990s, debates over who could claim Ivorian citizenship and participate in the nation's political life became increasingly contentious. These debates often revolved around questions of who was considered "truly Ivorian" and who was excluded.

The north-south divide in Côte d'Ivoire's politics and society became particularly pronounced. The northern regions of the country, home to ethnic groups like the Senufo and Malinké, felt marginalized and excluded from the political and economic center in the south. This division deepened ethnic tensions and contributed to periods of political instability.

The 2002 rebellion and subsequent periods of armed conflict were, in part, fueled by ethnic and regional grievances. The nation's political landscape became polarized along north-south lines, leading to a protracted period of instability and violence.

Efforts to address the challenges of ethnic diversity and forge national unity have been ongoing. Various peace agreements and reconciliation processes have been initiated to heal the divisions and bring stability to the country. These efforts have sought to build bridges between different ethnic and regional communities and promote social cohesion.

In recent years, steps have been taken to address issues related to citizenship and identity. National dialogues and reforms have aimed to create a more inclusive and equitable framework for Ivorian citizenship, reducing the potential for ethnic-based discrimination.

Côte d'Ivoire's journey toward national unity remains a complex and ongoing process. The challenges posed by ethnic diversity are not easily overcome, but the nation's history has shown that it is possible to find common ground and build a shared Ivorian identity that transcends ethnic affiliations. As Côte d'Ivoire continues to navigate these challenges, the pursuit of national unity remains a central aspiration for the nation and its people.

The Ivorian Miracle: Economic Growth

Côte d'Ivoire's economic trajectory, often referred to as the "Ivorian Miracle," is a compelling story of remarkable economic growth and development. The nation's journey from a post-independence economy heavily dependent on agriculture to a dynamic and diversified economy has captured the attention of economists and policymakers alike.

The early years of independence were marked by President Félix Houphouët-Boigny's vision for economic development. He recognized the potential of Côte d'Ivoire's abundant natural resources, particularly cocoa and coffee, and embarked on a path of economic transformation.

One of the key drivers of the Ivorian Miracle was the government's commitment to agriculture. Cocoa and coffee, known as the nation's "brown gold" and "black gold," respectively, became central to the Ivorian economy. The government introduced policies and incentives to boost production, leading to significant increases in yields and exports.

Côte d'Ivoire's cocoa production, in particular, soared to unprecedented levels. It consistently ranked as the world's largest cocoa producer, providing a substantial share of global cocoa beans. The revenues generated from cocoa exports served as a critical source of income for the nation.

Coffee, too, played a significant role in the Ivorian

economy. Ivorian coffee, known for its quality, found its place in international markets, contributing to the nation's export earnings. The coffee sector added diversity to the country's agricultural exports, reducing dependence on a single commodity.

The Ivorian government also invested in infrastructure development. Roads, ports, and educational institutions were built to modernize the nation and improve transportation and access to education. This infrastructure development facilitated trade, making it easier to transport goods to domestic and international markets.

Industrialization was another key component of the Ivorian Miracle. The government sought to add value to its agricultural products by processing them domestically. Cocoa and coffee processing industries emerged, creating employment opportunities and increasing the value of these commodities.

Additionally, Côte d'Ivoire's diversification efforts extended beyond agriculture. The nation's oil and gas sector witnessed significant growth, contributing to export revenues. Manufacturing industries expanded, producing a range of goods for both domestic consumption and export.

The Ivorian Miracle was also characterized by macroeconomic stability. The government pursued prudent fiscal policies and sought to attract foreign investment. This stability provided an attractive environment for both domestic and international investors.

Education and human capital development were prioritized as well. Investments in education and healthcare aimed to improve the well-being of the Ivorian people and create a skilled workforce to support the nation's economic growth.

While the Ivorian Miracle brought significant economic progress, it was not without its challenges. Income inequality persisted, and disparities in access to basic services remained a concern. Political stability was periodically tested, and the nation experienced periods of civil unrest and political strife.

The 1990s were marked by political and economic challenges, including a period of economic decline and social unrest. However, Côte d'Ivoire rebounded in the 2000s, experiencing a period of renewed economic growth and infrastructure development.

In recent years, Côte d'Ivoire has continued to prioritize economic diversification and regional integration. Initiatives aimed at reducing poverty, improving governance, and promoting inclusive growth have been central to the nation's development agenda.

The Ivorian Miracle, while a testament to the nation's resilience and potential, is an ongoing story. As Côte d'Ivoire navigates the complexities of a changing global economy and seeks to address remaining challenges, its journey toward sustained and inclusive economic growth continues to captivate observers and inspire hope for a prosperous future.

The Ivorian Civil War: A Nation Divided

The Ivorian Civil War, which unfolded from 2002 to 2007, stands as a painful chapter in Côte d'Ivoire's history, marked by political turmoil, violence, and a divided nation. It was a complex conflict rooted in long-standing ethnic, political, and economic tensions that would have far-reaching consequences for the nation and its people.

The origins of the Ivorian Civil War can be traced back to the 1990s, a period marked by economic decline, political unrest, and social dissatisfaction. Political opposition to President Félix Houphouët-Boigny's one-party rule had been growing for some time, and his death in 1993 marked a period of political transition.

The 2000 presidential election was a pivotal moment in Côte d'Ivoire's political landscape. Laurent Gbagbo, leader of the Ivorian Popular Front (FPI), and Alassane Ouattara, an economist and former Prime Minister, were the main contenders. The election became a catalyst for the ethnic and political divisions that would eventually lead to the civil war.

The election's outcome was marred by controversy and allegations of fraud, resulting in a disputed presidency. Laurent Gbagbo claimed victory, but the international community, led by the United Nations and African Union, recognized Alassane Ouattara as the legitimate winner.

The country became effectively divided, with Gbagbo

retaining control over the south, including the economic capital, Abidjan, and Ouattara leading a rebel faction in the north. This north-south divide deepened ethnic and regional tensions, pitting different communities against each other.

The civil war officially began in September 2002 when rebel forces, known as the New Forces or Forces Nouvelles, launched an uprising against the government. This rebellion aimed to overthrow Gbagbo's regime and establish control over the entire country. The conflict quickly escalated, leading to widespread violence and displacement.

The international community, including French and UN forces, attempted to broker peace agreements and mediate the conflict. Various peace accords were signed, but they often proved fragile, and violence would flare up again. The division of the country into a government-controlled south and rebel-held north persisted for years.

During the civil war, Côte d'Ivoire experienced economic stagnation and decline. The conflict disrupted agricultural activities, particularly in the cocoa-producing regions, leading to a significant drop in cocoa production. This, in turn, had a detrimental impact on the nation's economy.

The civil war also had a devastating humanitarian toll. Thousands of people were killed, and many more were displaced from their homes. Ethnic and political violence led to deep-seated animosities between different communities, further complicating the prospects for reconciliation.

The conflict reached a turning point in 2007 when a peace agreement led to a power-sharing arrangement between

Laurent Gbagbo and Alassane Ouattara. This arrangement aimed to end the violence and move toward national reconciliation. However, it would take several more years and international intervention, including a UN peacekeeping mission, to stabilize the country.

The Ivorian Civil War officially came to an end in 2007, but the scars of the conflict remained. The nation faced the immense challenge of rebuilding and reconciling a deeply divided society. Truth and reconciliation processes were initiated, and efforts were made to address the root causes of the conflict, including issues of citizenship and identity.

Despite the challenges, Côte d'Ivoire made significant progress in the years following the civil war. Alassane Ouattara was officially inaugurated as president in 2011, and the nation embarked on a path of economic recovery and political stabilization.

The Ivorian Civil War serves as a sobering reminder of the complexities and consequences of ethnic, political, and economic divisions. While the conflict has left a lasting legacy of pain and division, it has also motivated efforts to build a more inclusive and peaceful future for Côte d'Ivoire, with the hope that the nation can emerge stronger and more united from the scars of its past.

Post-Conflict Recovery: Reconciliation Efforts

In the aftermath of the Ivorian Civil War, Côte d'Ivoire faced the daunting task of rebuilding a fractured nation and fostering reconciliation among its deeply divided communities. The wounds of the conflict ran deep, and the scars of violence and displacement were still fresh. However, the Ivorian people, along with the support of the international community, embarked on a journey of healing, reconciliation, and recovery.

One of the first steps toward post-conflict recovery was the restoration of political stability. The power-sharing arrangement between Laurent Gbagbo and Alassane Ouattara, which culminated in Ouattara's presidency, provided a degree of political stability that had been lacking for years. The international community, through the United Nations Operation in Côte d'Ivoire (UNOCI), played a crucial role in maintaining this stability and supporting the political transition.

Reconciliation efforts focused on multiple fronts, including truth and reconciliation processes, disarmament, demobilization, and reintegration (DDR) programs, and the promotion of national dialogue. Truth and reconciliation commissions were established to investigate human rights abuses and provide a platform for victims and perpetrators to share their stories. These commissions sought to uncover the truth about the conflict and foster understanding among different communities.

The DDR programs aimed to reintegrate former combatants into civilian life, providing them with opportunities for education, vocational training, and employment. These programs were critical in preventing a return to violence by offering former fighters an alternative path.

National dialogue initiatives brought together representatives from various political, ethnic, and social groups to discuss the root causes of the conflict and chart a path toward national unity. These dialogues were instrumental in building bridges between communities and addressing grievances.

Another key aspect of post-conflict recovery was the reestablishment of the rule of law and justice. The International Criminal Court (ICC) issued arrest warrants for individuals accused of committing war crimes and crimes against humanity during the civil war, contributing to accountability for past atrocities.

Economic recovery was also a central concern. The conflict had disrupted economic activities, particularly in the agriculture sector, which was vital to the nation's economy. Efforts were made to revitalize agriculture, with a focus on rehabilitating cocoa and coffee farms, promoting small-scale farming, and enhancing access to credit for farmers.

The international community played a significant role in supporting Côte d'Ivoire's post-conflict recovery. Peacekeeping missions, humanitarian assistance, and financial aid were crucial in stabilizing the country and financing recovery programs.

Despite the progress made, challenges remained. The wounds of the civil war were not easily healed, and mistrust among different communities lingered. Political tensions persisted, and there were periodic outbreaks of violence. Building a culture of reconciliation and tolerance required time and sustained effort.

Côte d'Ivoire's journey toward reconciliation and recovery was also intertwined with the 2010-2011 post-electoral crisis, which further tested the nation's resilience. However, the eventual resolution of the crisis and the inauguration of Alassane Ouattara as president signaled a commitment to moving forward.

In recent years, Côte d'Ivoire has made significant strides in its post-conflict recovery. The nation's economy has rebounded, and infrastructure development has continued. Efforts to promote national unity, social cohesion, and inclusivity have been ongoing, with the hope of preventing a recurrence of the violence that marked the civil war.

The story of Côte d'Ivoire's post-conflict recovery serves as a testament to the resilience of its people and their determination to overcome the challenges of a divided past. While the road to reconciliation and healing may be long and arduous, it is a journey guided by the hope of a brighter and more united future for the nation and its citizens.

Laurent Gbagbo and the Ivorian Crisis

Laurent Gbagbo, a prominent figure in Ivorian politics, played a pivotal role in the turbulent history of Côte d'Ivoire, especially during the period of the Ivorian Crisis. His leadership, marked by political maneuvering, ethnic tensions, and contested elections, left a profound impact on the nation and its people.

Laurent Gbagbo's rise to power can be traced back to his involvement in the Ivorian opposition during the 1990s. As a leader of the Ivorian Popular Front (FPI), Gbagbo emerged as a prominent figure in the political landscape, advocating for democratic reforms and challenging the one-party rule of President Félix Houphouët-Boigny.

The 2000 presidential election marked a turning point in Gbagbo's political career. He contested the election as the FPI candidate, and the outcome was hotly disputed. Gbagbo claimed victory, but allegations of electoral fraud and international scrutiny marred the process. This disputed election laid the foundation for the political turmoil that would grip Côte d'Ivoire for years to come.

The international community, including the United Nations and African Union, recognized Alassane Ouattara as the legitimate winner of the election. Gbagbo's refusal to step down and hand over power led to a protracted political standoff that would escalate into the Ivorian Crisis.

The crisis reached its peak in 2002 when rebel forces,

known as the New Forces or Forces Nouvelles, launched an uprising against Gbagbo's government. This rebellion aimed to topple Gbagbo and take control of the country. The ensuing civil war resulted in violence, displacement, and a deepening division between the north and south of the country.

During the crisis, Laurent Gbagbo remained a central figure in Ivorian politics. He enjoyed support from segments of the Ivorian population, particularly in the southern regions, where he maintained control. Gbagbo's leadership was characterized by nationalist rhetoric and defiance in the face of international pressure to cede power.

The international community, including the United Nations and France, sought to mediate the conflict and find a peaceful resolution. Various peace agreements were brokered, but they often proved fragile, and violence would flare up again.

The crisis persisted for years, with intermittent periods of violence and instability. The nation's economy suffered, and its social fabric was deeply strained. The north-south divide, ethnic tensions, and political animosities remained significant obstacles to peace.

In 2010, another presidential election further escalated the crisis. Laurent Gbagbo and Alassane Ouattara both claimed victory, leading to a post-electoral crisis that threatened to plunge the country into further chaos. The standoff between the two rivals culminated in a violent conflict that lasted for several months.

International intervention, including a United Nations peacekeeping mission and military support for Ouattara's forces, eventually led to Gbagbo's capture in April 2011. He was arrested and later transferred to the International Criminal Court (ICC) to face charges of war crimes and crimes against humanity.

Gbagbo's arrest marked a turning point in the Ivorian Crisis. Alassane Ouattara was inaugurated as president, and the nation embarked on a path of political stabilization, post-conflict recovery, and reconciliation.

Laurent Gbagbo's legacy in Côte d'Ivoire is a complex and contentious one. While he retained support from a segment of the population, especially in the south, his leadership was also associated with a period of political turmoil, violence, and division. The Ivorian Crisis, characterized by contested elections and civil conflict, left a lasting impact on the nation, one that Côte d'Ivoire continues to grapple with as it seeks to rebuild and heal.

Ivory Coast in the 21st Century: A New Dawn

The 21st century ushered in a new era for Côte d'Ivoire, a period marked by profound changes, challenges, and opportunities. After years of political turmoil, conflict, and division, the nation embarked on a journey of reconstruction, reconciliation, and renewal.

The early years of the 21st century were characterized by post-conflict recovery efforts. Alassane Ouattara, officially inaugurated as president in 2011, faced the daunting task of rebuilding a country torn apart by years of civil war and political strife. The scars of the Ivorian Crisis were still visible, but there was a palpable sense of hope that a brighter future lay ahead.

One of the immediate priorities was restoring stability and security. The United Nations peacekeeping mission, UNOCI, played a crucial role in maintaining peace and supporting the Ivorian government in its efforts to disarm former combatants and reintegrate them into civilian life.

Economic recovery was another central focus. The government sought to revitalize key sectors of the economy, including agriculture, by rehabilitating cocoa and coffee farms, investing in infrastructure, and promoting foreign investment. Côte d'Ivoire's cocoa production rebounded, reaffirming its position as the world's largest cocoa producer.

The nation's economic diversification efforts extended

beyond agriculture. The oil and gas sector continued to grow, contributing to export revenues. Manufacturing industries expanded, and infrastructure development projects, including roads and ports, aimed to modernize the country and improve transportation networks.

Reconciliation and healing were ongoing priorities. Truth and reconciliation commissions sought to address the legacy of the civil war, provide a platform for victims and perpetrators to share their stories, and foster understanding among different communities. National dialogue initiatives aimed to bridge ethnic and political divides and promote national unity.

Côte d'Ivoire also faced the challenge of addressing issues related to citizenship and identity, which had been contentious during the Ivorian Crisis. Efforts to create a more inclusive and equitable framework for Ivorian citizenship were initiated to reduce the potential for ethnic-based discrimination.

The nation's political landscape continued to evolve. Multi-party democracy was reinstated, and presidential and legislative elections were held, further solidifying the country's commitment to democratic governance. However, the legacy of political divisions and contested elections remained a part of the nation's history.

In the realm of international relations, Côte d'Ivoire actively engaged with regional and global partners. The nation sought to strengthen economic ties, promote regional integration, and play a constructive role in addressing regional challenges. Côte d'Ivoire's participation in regional organizations, such as the Economic Community of West African States (ECOWAS), reflected its commitment to regional cooperation and stability.

While progress had been made in many areas, challenges persisted. Income inequality remained a concern, and disparities in access to basic services were still present. The process of reconciliation and building a culture of tolerance and inclusivity was ongoing and required sustained effort.

Côte d'Ivoire's journey into the 21st century was a testament to the resilience of its people and their determination to overcome the challenges of a divided past. The nation's ability to navigate the complexities of post-conflict recovery and renewal was a source of inspiration and hope for the future.

As the 21st century unfolded, Côte d'Ivoire stood at a crossroads, poised to embrace its potential and contribute to the prosperity and stability of the West African region. The Ivorian people looked forward to a future that held the promise of unity, development, and a new dawn for their nation.

Wildlife Wonders: Biodiversity in Ivory Coast

Côte d'Ivoire, with its diverse ecosystems and varied landscapes, is home to a rich tapestry of wildlife and biodiversity. From lush rainforests to savannas and coastal wetlands, the country's natural habitats provide shelter to an impressive array of flora and fauna, making it a wildlife enthusiast's paradise.

The rainforests of Côte d'Ivoire, particularly those in the southwest, are renowned for their incredible biodiversity. These forests are part of the Upper Guinean Forests, a globally significant biodiversity hotspot. Within these dense canopies, a treasure trove of plant and animal species thrives.

One of the most iconic residents of the Ivorian rainforests is the chimpanzee (Pan troglodytes). These intelligent primates are found in protected areas like Taï National Park, where researchers have conducted extensive studies on their behavior and social structures.

Another remarkable primate species found in Côte d'Ivoire is the Diana monkey (Cercopithecus diana), known for its striking black and white fur and distinctive facial markings. These monkeys inhabit the forests of the Taï region and are a delight for wildlife enthusiasts and researchers alike.

In the coastal and mangrove regions of Côte d'Ivoire, one can encounter the West African manatee (Trichechus senegalensis), a gentle and elusive marine mammal. These herbivores are known for their slow movements and inhabit the country's lagoons, estuaries, and rivers.

Birdwatchers are in for a treat in Côte d'Ivoire, as the nation boasts an impressive avian diversity. The country is home to over 700 bird species, making it a paradise for ornithologists. In the Comoé National Park, one can spot the rare and endangered Egyptian plover (Pluvianus aegyptius), known for its striking appearance and distinctive breeding behavior.

Côte d'Ivoire's grassy savannas are inhabited by numerous large mammals, including the African elephant (Loxodonta africana). These majestic creatures roam protected areas like Comoé National Park and Marahoué National Park. Additionally, African lions (Panthera leo) and leopards (Panthera pardus) are also found in the savanna regions, albeit in smaller numbers.

In the coastal and marine ecosystems, the hawksbill sea turtle (Eretmochelys imbricata) is a critically endangered species that nest along the Ivorian shores. Conservation efforts are underway to protect these nesting sites and ensure the survival of this magnificent sea turtle species.

Côte d'Ivoire's marine waters are also teeming with diverse marine life. From colorful coral reefs to a plethora of fish species, the country's coastal areas offer fantastic opportunities for snorkeling and diving. The Abidjan National Park, established to protect marine biodiversity, is a testament to the nation's commitment to conserving its coastal ecosystems.

The government of Côte d'Ivoire, along with various conservation organizations, has recognized the importance of preserving this extraordinary biodiversity. Protected areas like Taï National Park, Marahoué National Park, Comoé National Park, and many others have been established to safeguard the natural habitats of these remarkable species.

Efforts to combat illegal wildlife trade, habitat loss, and poaching are ongoing to ensure the long-term survival of these unique creatures. By promoting eco-tourism and sustainable practices, Côte d'Ivoire aims to strike a balance between economic development and biodiversity conservation, offering a glimpse into the fascinating world of wildlife wonders that call this beautiful nation home.

Savory Delights: Ivorian Cuisine

Côte d'Ivoire, a land of vibrant cultures and diverse traditions, boasts a rich and flavorful culinary heritage. Ivorian cuisine is a delightful fusion of indigenous ingredients, traditional cooking techniques, and influences from various ethnic groups, making it a gastronomic journey filled with savory delights.

At the heart of Ivorian cuisine lies the staple food, which is typically a starchy base such as rice, maize, cassava, yam, or plantains. These starchy foods provide the foundation for a wide range of savory dishes, each with its unique flavor profile and regional variations.

One of the most beloved Ivorian dishes is "Foutou," a smooth and elastic dough made from cassava or yam. Foutou is often served with delectable sauces, and it's customary to eat it with the fingers, using it to scoop up the sauce.

Another Ivorian favorite is "Attieke," a couscous-like side dish made from fermented cassava. Attieke is light and fluffy, often served with grilled or fried fish, chicken, or spicy sauces, creating a harmonious combination of flavors and textures.

"Garba," a popular dish in the northern regions, features millet or maize balls served with a savory sauce, usually made from groundnuts. The unique combination of grains and nutty flavors makes Garba a distinctive culinary experience.

Ivorian cuisine also showcases a variety of flavorful soups and stews. "Kedjenou" is a slow-cooked chicken stew prepared with vegetables, spices, and palm oil. The slow simmering allows the flavors to meld together, resulting in a mouthwatering and tender dish.

"Poulet Bicyclette," or "bicycle chicken," is a grilled chicken dish often sold by street vendors. Marinated with spices and herbs, this grilled chicken is a tantalizing treat for those seeking a savory snack on the go.

Seafood lovers will find a haven in Côte d'Ivoire's coastal regions. Freshly caught fish, prawns, and crabs are expertly prepared and served in a variety of ways, from grilled to fried and stewed in aromatic sauces.

"Kedjenou de Poisson," a fish version of the classic Kedjenou, showcases the coastal influence with its use of fish, vegetables, and spices slow-cooked in a clay pot, allowing the flavors to infuse the fish beautifully.

For those with a penchant for spicier fare, "Choukouya" is a popular street food snack. It features grilled and spiced meat, often served on skewers, and is a delightful blend of smoky, spicy, and savory flavors.

Côte d'Ivoire's tropical climate also blesses the nation with an abundance of fruits, including bananas, pineapples, papayas, and mangoes. These fruits are enjoyed fresh or incorporated into desserts and beverages, adding a sweet and refreshing touch to the cuisine.

Ivorian desserts, while not as prominent as savory dishes, offer a satisfying conclusion to a meal. "Chinchinga" is a sweet fried doughnut that's hard to resist, often enjoyed with a cup of tea or coffee.

To wash down the delectable Ivorian dishes, one can savor "Bissap," a refreshing hibiscus flower drink sweetened with sugar and sometimes infused with ginger for an extra kick.

Ivorian cuisine is not just about the food; it's a cultural expression that reflects the nation's history, diversity, and the warmth of its people. Whether savoring a traditional meal in a local village or exploring the vibrant culinary scene of Abidjan, Côte d'Ivoire invites you to embark on a savory journey that celebrates the flavors of this beautiful West African nation.

Grand-Bassam: Colonial Gem by the Sea

Grand-Bassam, with its serene coastal beauty and rich historical significance, stands as a testament to Côte d'Ivoire's colonial past. This picturesque town, nestled along the Gulf of Guinea, holds a unique place in the nation's history and offers a captivating glimpse into a bygone era.

Founded in the mid-19th century by the French colonial authorities, Grand-Bassam served as the first capital of Côte d'Ivoire, then known as the French colony of Ivory Coast. Its strategic location along the coast made it an ideal hub for trade and administration, connecting the colonial powers with the interior of West Africa.

The town's architecture reflects the colonial influence, characterized by charming colonial-era buildings with distinctive verandas, shuttered windows, and ornate balconies. The historic architecture is a blend of French colonial styles, including elements of Creole, neo-Gothic, and neo-Romanesque designs, giving Grand-Bassam a unique and timeless charm.

One of the iconic landmarks of Grand-Bassam is the Assini Prudhomme Bridge, a beautiful iron bridge constructed in the early 20th century. This bridge not only serves as a functional crossing over the Comoé River but also stands as a symbol of the town's enduring history.

Grand-Bassam's historic center, known as the "Cours

Bertin," is a designated UNESCO World Heritage Site, recognized for its cultural significance and architectural heritage. Strolling through its cobblestone streets, visitors can explore the old colonial administrative buildings, including the former governor's residence, which now houses the National Costume Museum.

The town's serene beaches, fringed with palm trees and lapped by the warm waters of the Gulf of Guinea, have made it a popular destination for both locals and tourists. The beaches of Grand-Bassam offer a tranquil escape, where one can relax, swim, or simply enjoy the breathtaking coastal views.

Grand-Bassam's connection to history extends to its role in the African and global trade networks during the colonial era. The town was a center for the export of commodities such as palm oil, rubber, cocoa, and timber, which were transported to Europe through its bustling port.

The town's history is not without its challenges, as Grand-Bassam faced the impacts of colonial rule, including forced labor and exploitation. However, it also witnessed the resilience and resistance of its people, who played a vital role in the struggle for independence.

In the mid-20th century, as Côte d'Ivoire gained independence, the capital was relocated to Abidjan, leaving Grand-Bassam as a historical gem frozen in time. Today, the town stands as a living museum, preserving the legacy of its colonial past and inviting visitors to immerse themselves in its enchanting ambiance.

Grand-Bassam's cultural heritage is celebrated through various events and festivals, including the annual Grand-

Bassam Cultural Week, where traditional music, dance, and art take center stage. This vibrant cultural scene reflects the town's enduring spirit and the resilience of its people.

As Grand-Bassam continues to evolve, efforts are made to preserve its historical charm while promoting tourism and economic development. The town's cultural significance and architectural splendor make it a destination that captivates the imagination, offering a window into the colonial history of Côte d'Ivoire and the enduring legacy of Grand-Bassam as a coastal gem by the sea.

Abidjan: The Economic Capital

Abidjan, often referred to as the "Paris of West Africa," stands as the economic capital and a vibrant metropolis of Côte d'Ivoire. This sprawling urban center, situated along the picturesque Ébrié Lagoon, is a testament to the nation's economic dynamism, cultural diversity, and cosmopolitan spirit.

The rise of Abidjan as Côte d'Ivoire's economic hub can be traced back to the country's post-independence era. When the capital was moved from Grand-Bassam to Abidjan in 1933, it marked the beginning of a transformational journey for the city. The decision to relocate the capital was driven by Abidjan's strategic location, offering access to both the Atlantic Ocean and the interior regions of the country.

Today, Abidjan is a bustling city that serves as a major economic gateway to West Africa. The city's modern skyline, adorned with skyscrapers and architectural marvels, reflects its status as a regional economic powerhouse. Its central business district, Plateau, hosts the headquarters of numerous national and international corporations, financial institutions, and government agencies.

The Port of Abidjan, one of Africa's largest and busiest seaports, plays a pivotal role in the country's economy. It serves as a vital transportation hub, facilitating the import and export of goods not only for Côte d'Ivoire but also for neighboring landlocked countries in the West African region.

Abidjan's economy is diverse, encompassing a wide range of sectors. The city is a center for banking and finance, with the presence of major national and international banks. Additionally, Abidjan's industrial base includes food processing, textiles, chemicals, and manufacturing, contributing significantly to the nation's industrial output.

Côte d'Ivoire's robust agricultural sector also plays a crucial role in Abidjan's economy. The city is home to the world's largest cocoa bean market, a testament to the country's status as a leading cocoa producer. The cocoa trade is a cornerstone of the Ivorian economy, and Abidjan's ports facilitate the export of cocoa and other agricultural products to global markets.

Abidjan's transportation infrastructure is well-developed, with an extensive road network, bridges, and a commuter rail system. The Félix Houphouët-Boigny International Airport, named after the country's founding president, is the nation's largest and busiest airport, connecting Abidjan to numerous international destinations.

The city's cultural vibrancy is a reflection of its rich ethnic diversity. Abidjan is a melting pot of cultures, home to various ethnic groups from across Côte d'Ivoire and the broader West African region. This diversity is celebrated through music, dance, cuisine, and festivals, making Abidjan a dynamic and culturally rich metropolis.

Abidjan's nightlife is legendary in West Africa. The city comes alive after dark, with a thriving entertainment scene that includes nightclubs, live music venues, and restaurants offering a diverse range of culinary experiences. Music genres like Coupe-Decale, a popular Ivorian music style, have their roots in Abidjan and resonate throughout the city.

The city's education and healthcare infrastructure is well-developed, with prestigious universities, research institutions, and modern medical facilities. Abidjan attracts students and professionals from across the continent and beyond.

Abidjan's natural beauty is complemented by its coastal location, offering residents and visitors access to stunning beaches, water sports, and recreational activities along the Ébrié Lagoon and the Atlantic coastline.

Despite its economic prosperity and urban development, Abidjan faces challenges such as urban sprawl, traffic congestion, and issues related to waste management and sanitation. However, the city's government and residents are actively working to address these challenges and ensure sustainable urban growth.

Abidjan is a city that continues to evolve, driven by its dynamic economy, cultural richness, and the resilience of its people. It represents the spirit of progress and opportunity that defines Côte d'Ivoire and stands as a beacon of hope and aspiration for the nation and the region as a whole.

Yamoussoukro: City of the Basilica

Yamoussoukro, the political capital of Côte d'Ivoire, is a city steeped in history and cultural significance. Its claim to fame lies in the majestic Basilica of Our Lady of Peace of Yamoussoukro, one of the largest churches in the world, which dominates the cityscape and draws visitors from far and wide.

The story of Yamoussoukro's transformation into the political capital of Côte d'Ivoire is intrinsically linked to its most iconic landmark, the Basilica. The dream of building this grand church was conceived by Félix Houphouët-Boigny, the nation's founding father and first president. Houphouët-Boigny, born in Yamoussoukro, envisioned a symbol of peace and unity that would not only serve as a place of worship but also as a testament to his vision for the nation.

Construction of the Basilica began in 1986 and was completed in 1989, making it one of the most ambitious architectural endeavors of the 20th century. The Basilica's design draws inspiration from the Vatican's St. Peter's Basilica in Rome and showcases a stunning blend of neo-Gothic and neo-Baroque architectural styles. Its central dome, soaring 158 meters (518 feet) into the sky, is adorned with a massive cross, creating a breathtaking spectacle. The interior of the Basilica is equally impressive, with a cavernous nave capable of accommodating thousands of worshipers. The marble-clad floors, intricate stained glass windows, and ornate sculptures and artwork contribute to the church's grandeur. The Basilica's organ, with thousands of pipes, adds to the spiritual experience during religious services and concerts. The Basilica of Our Lady of Peace was consecrated by Pope John Paul II in 1990 during a historic visit to Côte d'Ivoire. This momentous occasion solidified the church's status as a globally recognized place of worship and pilgrimage.

Yamoussoukro's transformation did not end with the construction of the Basilica. The city underwent extensive infrastructure development to accommodate the nation's political functions. Government buildings, foreign embassies, and diplomatic residences were established, making Yamoussoukro the official political capital while Abidjan remained the economic capital.

Despite its prominent status, Yamoussoukro is often described as a quiet and tranquil city, in stark contrast to the bustling urban energy of Abidjan. The city's streets are lined with lush vegetation, creating a serene atmosphere that complements the grandeur of the Basilica.

While the Basilica is the city's centerpiece, Yamoussoukro also boasts other attractions. The Houphouët-Boigny Foundation, dedicated to the nation's first president, is a cultural and historical center that offers insights into the life and legacy of Félix Houphouët-Boigny.

Yamoussoukro serves as a testament to the vision of its founder and the enduring legacy of the Basilica. It remains a destination for religious pilgrims, tourists, and those seeking a moment of tranquility and reflection within the awe-inspiring walls of the Basilica of Our Lady of Peace. The city's unique status as both a political capital and a spiritual center continues to shape its identity and contribute to the cultural fabric of Côte d'Ivoire.

Gagnoa: The Birthplace of Houphouët-Boigny

Gagnoa, a city nestled in the heart of Côte d'Ivoire, holds a special place in the nation's history as the birthplace of Félix Houphouët-Boigny, the founding father and first president of the country. The city's significance transcends its geographical location; it is a place of historical, cultural, and political importance, intimately tied to the life and legacy of this iconic leader.

Félix Houphouët-Boigny was born on October 18, 1905, in Gagnoa, then a small village in the French colony of Ivory Coast. His early years were marked by humble beginnings, growing up in a traditional African setting where he learned the customs and values of his ethnic group, the Baulé.

As a young man, Houphouët-Boigny left Gagnoa to pursue higher education in Senegal and France, where he studied medicine and became a successful physician. His time abroad exposed him to political ideologies and activism, igniting a passion for African independence and self-determination.

Returning to his homeland, Houphouët-Boigny began his political career, advocating for the rights and interests of the Ivorian people. He played a pivotal role in Ivory Coast's transition to independence from French colonial rule, culminating in the country's sovereignty in 1960.

Gagnoa remained close to Houphouët-Boigny's heart throughout his life. He often visited the city, staying connected to his roots and the people who had witnessed his journey from a small village to the halls of international diplomacy. His enduring commitment to Gagnoa was reflected in the development projects he initiated in the city, including infrastructure improvements, education facilities, and healthcare services.

One of Gagnoa's enduring symbols is the Félix Houphouët-Boigny Stadium, named in honor of the city's most famous son. The stadium serves as a reminder of his dedication to sports and physical education as means of fostering national unity and pride.

Gagnoa's cultural heritage is deeply intertwined with the Baulé traditions, and the city's residents continue to celebrate their ethnic identity through music, dance, and art. The vibrant Baulé culture is showcased during various festivals and ceremonies, preserving the rich cultural tapestry of the region.

The city's agricultural landscape is characterized by lush vegetation, with cocoa, coffee, and palm plantations dotting the surrounding countryside. These crops are not only essential to the local economy but also represent Ivorian staples and exports that have contributed to the nation's economic growth.

Gagnoa's proximity to the lush forests of the interior makes it a gateway to the natural beauty and biodiversity that characterize Côte d'Ivoire. The city's surroundings offer opportunities for eco-tourism, attracting nature enthusiasts and wildlife lovers to explore the untamed landscapes of the region.

In essence, Gagnoa stands as a testament to the

transformative journey of Félix Houphouët-Boigny and the enduring connection between an individual and his birthplace. The city's historical significance, cultural richness, and agricultural heritage contribute to its identity as a place of pride for the people of Côte d'Ivoire. Gagnoa continues to honor the memory of its most illustrious native, preserving his legacy and the values he held dear, while also embracing the promise of progress and development in the modern era.

Man and the Dan Culture: A Window to the Past

Nestled in the western part of Côte d'Ivoire lies the town of Man, a place of rich cultural significance and a gateway to the unique heritage of the Dan people. Man, often referred to as the "City of Eight Mountains" due to its picturesque setting amid a cluster of verdant peaks, serves as a living testament to the Dan culture, one of the most fascinating and distinctive in West Africa.

The Dan people, also known as the Yacouba, are an ethnic group with deep roots in this region. Their culture, traditions, and artistic expressions have captivated scholars, anthropologists, and art enthusiasts for decades, offering a glimpse into the complexities of pre-colonial African societies.

Central to the Dan culture is the practice of masquerade, which is an integral part of their social and religious life. Dan masks, known for their striking, abstract designs, are crafted with great skill and artistic prowess. These masks are used in various ceremonies, including initiations, funerals, and celebrations, and are believed to embody the spirits of the ancestors.

The use of masks in Dan culture goes beyond mere aesthetic expression; it is a means of communication with the spirit world. Each mask has its unique significance, and the way it is danced, worn, and displayed conveys specific messages or intentions. These masks are passed down through generations and hold immense cultural value.

Man and its surrounding villages are home to master mask makers and artisans who continue to create these remarkable works of art. Visitors to the region can witness the intricate process of mask carving, from selecting the right wood to meticulously shaping the mask and adorning it with natural pigments and materials.

The annual Fêtes des Masques, or Mask Festival, held in Man, is a highlight of the cultural calendar. During this vibrant celebration, Dan masks come to life as they are danced by skilled performers. The festival attracts both locals and tourists, providing an opportunity to experience the living traditions of the Dan people.

Beyond the realm of masquerades, the Dan culture is deeply rooted in agriculture. The region's fertile soil and favorable climate have historically supported the cultivation of crops such as yams, plantains, and cocoa. Agriculture remains a cornerstone of the Dan way of life, providing sustenance and livelihoods for the community.

The Dan people have a strong sense of communal living and social organization. Traditionally, their society is organized into clans and age-grade associations, each with its roles and responsibilities. These structures play a crucial role in maintaining social cohesion and order within the community.

As with many African cultures, storytelling is an essential aspect of Dan heritage. Oral traditions are passed down from one generation to the next, preserving the collective memory and wisdom of the Dan people. Stories, myths, and proverbs are used to convey lessons, morals, and the history of the community.

The landscape surrounding Man is a testament to the region's natural beauty and biodiversity. The picturesque mountains, lush forests, and cascading waterfalls make it a haven for eco-tourism and adventure seekers. The natural wonders of the region, such as Mount Tonkoui, attract hikers and nature enthusiasts from far and wide.

In conclusion, Man and the Dan culture offer a captivating window into the past, where tradition and modernity coexist harmoniously. The Dan people's deep connection to their heritage, their artistic expressions, and their reverence for the natural world make this region a remarkable and culturally rich destination within Côte d'Ivoire. As the world evolves, the Dan culture endures, serving as a reminder of the diversity and depth of African heritage.

Sassandra: Fishing and Beach Paradise

Sassandra, a coastal town nestled on the Gulf of Guinea in southwestern Côte d'Ivoire, is a hidden gem known for its pristine beaches, vibrant fishing culture, and laid-back atmosphere. As you approach Sassandra, the azure waters of the Atlantic Ocean greet you, inviting you into a world of natural beauty and cultural richness.

The town's economy is intricately tied to the sea, and fishing has been a way of life for generations of Sassandra's residents. Fishermen set out to sea in colorful wooden canoes, skillfully navigating the waves to bring back the day's catch. The fish market in Sassandra is a lively hub of activity, where the freshest seafood is bought and sold, connecting the ocean's bounty with the dinner tables of the town's inhabitants.

Sassandra's beaches are a sight to behold. The coastline stretches for miles, with golden sands gently caressed by the warm waters of the Atlantic. Coconut palms sway in the breeze, offering shade to beachgoers seeking respite from the sun's rays. The beaches are pristine and relatively untouched, providing a serene escape from the hustle and bustle of modern life.

One of the most famous beaches in Sassandra is Grand-Béréby Beach, located a short distance from the town center. This idyllic stretch of shoreline is a popular destination for both locals and tourists alike. The clear waters are perfect for swimming, and the beach offers opportunities for sunbathing, beach volleyball, and picnics. As the sun sets over the horizon, it paints the sky with hues of orange and pink, creating a breathtaking spectacle that draws visitors to the water's edge.

Sassandra's rich maritime heritage is on full display at the town's Musée Maritime, a small museum dedicated to preserving the history of the local fishing industry. Here, you can learn about the traditional fishing methods employed by the Dan people, the history of the town's port, and the cultural significance of fishing in Sassandra's society.

In addition to its natural beauty and fishing culture, Sassandra boasts a charming town center with colorful colonial-era buildings that exude a nostalgic ambiance. The town's architecture reflects its historical ties to French colonialism, adding to its unique character. Wandering through the narrow streets, you'll encounter lively marketplaces where local artisans sell their crafts and fresh produce.

Sassandra's culinary scene is a seafood lover's paradise. The town's restaurants and eateries serve up a delectable array of dishes featuring locally caught fish and seafood. From grilled barracuda to succulent lobster, the flavors of the ocean are celebrated in every bite.

Beyond its shores, Sassandra is surrounded by lush tropical rainforests and mangrove swamps that are home to a rich diversity of flora and fauna. Birdwatchers and nature enthusiasts can explore the nearby national parks and reserves, where the calls of exotic birds and the rustling of monkeys in the treetops create a symphony of sounds.

Sassandra is a town where time seems to slow down, and the simple pleasures of life take center stage. It offers a tranquil and authentic experience for those seeking to escape the frenetic pace of modern urban life. Whether you're lounging on the beach, savoring the local cuisine, or immersing yourself in the town's vibrant fishing culture, Sassandra is a coastal paradise that beckons travelers to explore its natural wonders and embrace its warm and welcoming spirit.

Comoe National Park: A Natural Treasure

Comoe National Park, situated in the northern part of Côte d'Ivoire, is a testament to the country's commitment to preserving its natural heritage. This expansive protected area, covering over 11,000 square kilometers (4,200 square miles), is not only one of the largest national parks in West Africa but also a biodiversity hotspot of global significance. Comoe National Park is a sanctuary where the untamed beauty of Africa's wilderness unfolds, offering a glimpse into the continent's ecological wonders.

One of the most remarkable features of Comoe National Park is its diverse range of habitats. Within its boundaries, you'll find a mosaic of landscapes, from savannahs and grasslands to dense forests and winding rivers. The park is crisscrossed by the Comoe River, which serves as a lifeline for both wildlife and local communities.

The wildlife in Comoe National Park is nothing short of extraordinary. It's home to an astonishing array of species, including some of Africa's most iconic animals. Elephants, the park's flagship species, roam freely in sizable herds, their presence a testament to the success of conservation efforts. Lions, leopards, cheetahs, and hyenas are among the predators that patrol the savannahs, while baboons, vervet monkeys, and chimpanzees thrive in the park's lush forests.

Bird enthusiasts will find their paradise in Comoe National Park, with over 300 species recorded. The park's wetlands and rivers attract a variety of waterfowl, including African fish eagles, kingfishers, and herons. The skies above the park are a canvas for vultures, raptors, and migratory birds, making it a birdwatcher's dream.

The waters of the Comoe River teem with life, including crocodiles, hippos, and numerous fish species. The riverbanks are also a haven for birdlife, and fishing communities along its shores have coexisted with the park's wildlife for generations, creating a unique cultural blend of human and natural heritage.

One of the park's unique features is the presence of "lansat" or "komoé," a type of savannah that provides crucial habitat for herbivores like antelopes, buffaloes, and warthogs. These animals, in turn, support the park's predators, creating a delicate balance in the ecosystem.

Comoe National Park's significance extends beyond its natural beauty. It has been designated a UNESCO World Heritage Site, recognizing its exceptional ecological value and its role in conserving endangered species. The park also plays a pivotal role in scientific research, with ongoing studies shedding light on African biodiversity and ecology.

Local communities living in and around Comoe National Park have cohabited with wildlife for generations. Their traditional knowledge of the land and its resources is invaluable in conservation efforts. Collaborative initiatives between park authorities and these communities seek to ensure the sustainable use of natural resources while also providing benefits to the people who call this region home.

Visitors to Comoe National Park have the opportunity to embark on safaris and guided tours that offer a chance to witness the park's wildlife in its natural habitat. The experience of observing elephants in the wild or encountering a rare bird species is both humbling and awe-inspiring.

As the challenges of conservation and sustainable development continue to evolve, Comoe National Park stands as a symbol of hope. It embodies the idea that humans can coexist harmoniously with nature, and that the protection of our natural heritage is not only an ethical responsibility but also a vital component of our collective future.

In the heart of West Africa, Comoe National Park beckons adventurers, nature lovers, and conservationists alike. Its sprawling landscapes, rich biodiversity, and cultural significance make it a true natural treasure and a testament to the beauty and resilience of Africa's wild places.

Conclusion

The history of Ivory Coast, or Côte d'Ivoire as it is officially known, is a tapestry woven with threads of ancient civilizations, rich cultures, and complex sociopolitical dynamics. As we conclude our journey through this fascinating nation's past and present, we find ourselves at a crossroads of reflection and contemplation.

From the early origins of human habitation in the region, where evidence of ancient societies and settlements date back thousands of years, to the emergence of powerful kingdoms like the Ghana Empire and the influence of trans-Saharan trade routes, Ivory Coast's history is a testament to the resilience and adaptability of its people.

The arrival of Islam and the subsequent interplay of faith and culture left an indelible mark on the nation, shaping the lives and beliefs of its inhabitants. The Akan and Baulé kingdoms along the coast, with their unique social structures and traditions, added further layers to Ivory Coast's diverse cultural mosaic.

The era of European exploration and the Portuguese connection opened up Ivory Coast to the wider world, setting the stage for the complex dynamics of trade and colonization. The impact of the transatlantic slave trade on the region's demographics and societies is a stark reminder of the harrowing legacy of that period.

The scramble for Africa, with France's arrival, ushered in a new chapter in Ivory Coast's history, one marked by colonial ambitions, economic exploitation, and cultural assimilation. The struggle for independence in the mid-20th century, led by iconic figures like Félix Houphouët-Boigny, marked a turning point in the nation's trajectory.

Ivory Coast's post-independence journey was marked by periods of political stability under one-party rule and significant economic growth driven by cocoa and coffee exports. However, challenges of ethnic diversity and national unity persisted, leading to moments of tension and conflict.

The Ivorian miracle of economic growth in the late 20th century was accompanied by growing pains, including ethnic and political strife that culminated in the Ivorian civil war, a dark chapter in the nation's history.

The efforts at post-conflict recovery and reconciliation are ongoing, symbolizing the resilience and determination of the Ivorian people to rebuild their nation and heal the wounds of the past.

In the 21st century, Ivory Coast has witnessed a new dawn, with efforts to strengthen democratic institutions and promote economic diversification. The nation's rich agricultural resources, including cocoa and coffee, continue to be pillars of its economy.

Challenges remain, but Ivory Coast's commitment to addressing them and embracing its diverse cultural heritage stands as a testament to its potential for a brighter future.

From the vibrant cities of Abidjan and Yamoussoukro to the colonial gems of Grand-Bassam and the cultural heartlands of Gagnoa and Man, Ivory Coast's cities and towns offer a kaleidoscope of experiences.

The natural wonders of Sassandra's beaches and Comoe National Park showcase the nation's breathtaking landscapes and biodiversity. Meanwhile, the culinary delights of Ivorian cuisine tantalize the taste buds, and the warm hospitality of its people leaves a lasting impression.

In closing, Ivory Coast's history is a story of resilience, diversity, and cultural richness. It is a nation that has weathered the storms of history, emerging stronger and more vibrant. As we bid adieu to this journey, may Ivory Coast continue to evolve and flourish, embracing the promise of a future filled with hope, unity, and prosperity.

Thank you for taking the time to read this book on the history and culture of Ivory Coast. I hope you found it informative, engaging, and enlightening. Your interest in this fascinating nation's story is greatly appreciated.

If you enjoyed this book and found it valuable, I kindly ask for your support in the form of a positive review. Your feedback is invaluable in helping others discover and appreciate the content within these pages.

Your review can make a significant difference in reaching a wider audience and encouraging more readers to explore the history, culture, and beauty of Ivory Coast. Thank you once again for your time and consideration, and I look forward to your thoughtful review.